Editor In Chief® products available in print or eBook form.

Beginning 1 • Beginning 2

Level 1 • Level 2 • Level 3

Written by

Cherie A. Plant

Nancy Rowe

Edited by

Patricia Gray

Graphic Design by

Scott Slyter

THE CRITICAL THINKING CO.™
www.CriticalThinking.com
Phone: 800-458-4849 • Fax: 541-756-1758
1991 Sherman Ave., Suite 200 • North Bend • OR 97459
ISBN 978-1-60144-766-1



Printed in the United States of America by Hatteras, Inc., Plymouth, MI (May 2025)

# Table of Contents

# About the Authors

## Cherie A. Plant

A graduate in Elementary Education with a minor in Latin from the City University of New York, Cherie Plant is an accomplished etymologist (one who studies the origin and derivation of words). While teaching, Plant found that children as young as seven were fascinated with decoding words such as "triskaidekaphobia" (fear of the number 13) using the knowledge of prefixes, suffixes, and root words.

Plant retired from teaching in 1995, but was convinced that other youngsters could benefit from such study. She has since devoted her time to writing language materials for all age groups, based on the study of Latin and Greek roots.

## Nancy Rowe

Nancy Rowe graduated from the University of Northern Colorado in Greeley, Colorado, with a Business Education major and minor in English. She also has a Masters in Elementary Reading. Rowe taught elementary education for 23 years. She worked in many areas of curriculum development to improve reading, math, and language arts. She retired in 2011 from the education field.

# To the Teacher

## Objective

*Editor in Chief® Level 2* teaches 12 lessons in grammar and mechanics. Students focus on one skill at a time and these lessons are:

1. Content
2. Capitalization
3. Punctuation
4. Spelling
5. Adjectives, Adverbs, Articles
6. Conjunctions, Prepositions, and Interjections
7. Pronouns
8. Verbs
9. Clauses and Phrases
10. Agreement
11. Confused Words/Negative Words
12. Run-On Sentences and Sentence Fragments

Students learn to apply these rules in context by correcting the errors in a variety of paragraphs. Following every three lessons, there is a mini review. In addition, Lessons 1-6 and 7-12 are followed by a review which provides more challenging practice of the multiple skills already taught. At the end, there is a final review of all the lessons.

## Rationale

The key difference between *Editor in Chief®* and most other grammar books is the focus on editing in context. The grammatical and mechanical errors inserted into the paragraphs are based on general instructional guidelines for specific grade levels; the content level, however, is ungraded, allowing usage of these materials at many instructional levels. Styles and content are varied to sustain interest and to broaden the students' exposure to different writing formats, such as letters, stories, and dialogue. The illustrations integrated into the context of the activities further spark student interest. The skills developed can be applied to the students' own writing.

## Activity

Each of the 12 lessons in *Editor in Chief® Level 2* is followed by four passages. The number of errors in the paragraphs varies and the students are asked to identify these errors. The number (in circles) and type of errors are shown to the right of each passage. Students may want to cross off the circles as they find the errors. Errors will be found in spelling, mechanics, and grammar related to each of the 12 lessons. Most corrections involve the insertion, modification, or deletion of punctuation marks, capitals, or single words within the text. There will also be errors pertaining to sentence structure. Students have the option to rewrite the passage without errors on a separate piece of paper.

## Answer Key

The answer key at the end of the book lists corrections for each passage. In some instances such as run-on sentences, the students may be able to correct an error in more than one way. The answer key gives the obvious choices, but the teacher may choose to accept other answers that make sense and are grammatically and mechanically correct.

## Teaching Suggestions

*Editor in Chief® Level 2* can be used as an individual or group activity for instruction, reinforcement, practice, and assessment of English grammar and mechanics. When introducing a new rule, several paragraphs can serve as an instructional example, and others as an assessment of a student's independent understanding. The mini-reviews and compilation reviews are designed to provide even more extensive opportunities to practice and reinforce the many skills developed throughout this book.

# Editing a Passage Lesson

Each passage contains errors. Find the errors and write the corrections as shown.

Read the passage and correct the errors. There are no errors in the picture or caption.

## Corn Palace

Mitchell, ~~North~~ South Dakota, is the home of the Corn Palace. This popular tourist attraction is visited by about half a million people each year. The walls of the Corn Palace exhibit beautiful murals. Scenes include birds in flight, Conestoga wagons heading West, Native American teepees, and rural settings. There is one peculiarity about these murals however, and that is that they are made out of corn, seeds, and grasses. The exterior murals are replaced each year with a new theme, partly because hungry birds eat from them. The original Corn Palace (known as The Corn Belt Exposition) was built in 1892 to showcase the rich soil of South ~~dakota~~ Dakota and to encourage people to settle in the area. At that time it was a simple wooden structure located on Mitchell's Main Street. Over the years, changes were made to the building which included the addition of such things as Moorish domes and minarets to give it the distinct ~~appearence~~ appearance that it has today.

This is a list of the errors in the passage.

- (1) Content
- (1) Capitalization
- (1) Punctuation
- (1) Spelling

The original Corn Palace was a simple wooden structure when it was built in 1892 in South Dakota.

- About one half of a million people visit it each year.
- The walls exhibit beautiful murals made of corn, seeds, and grasses.
- Today the building has Moorish domes and minarets.

# Lesson 1. Content

**Content** is all the information in a book, magazine, article, letter, passage, etc. This includes any graphics such as pictures, tables, and captions.

## Corn Palace

Mitchell, South Dakota, is the home of the Corn Palace. This popular tourist attraction is visited by about half a million people each year. The walls of the Corn Palace exhibit beautiful murals. Scenes include birds in flight, Conestoga wagons heading West, Native American teepees, and rural settings. There is one peculiarity about these murals however, and that is that they are made out of corn, seeds, and grasses. The exterior murals are replaced each year with a new theme, partly because hungry birds eat from them. The original Corn Palace (known as The Corn Belt Exposition) was built in 1892 to showcase the rich soil of South Dakota and to encourage people to settle in the area. At that time it was a simple wooden structure located on Mitchell's Main Street. Over the years, changes were made to the building which included the addition of such things as Moorish domes and minarets to give it the distinct appearance that it has today.

The original Corn Palace was a simple wooden structure when it was built in 1892 in South Dakota.

- About one half of a million people visit it each year.
- The walls exhibit beautiful murals made of corn, seeds, and grasses.
- Today the building has Moorish domes and minarets.

Read the passage and correct the content errors. There are no errors in the picture or caption.

## 1. On a Grand Scale

The ancient Egyptian architects built on a grand scale. Their greatest achievement was the pyramids. In comparison to modern structures, the pyramids were relatively tall in height but small in volume. These pyramids were constructed as tombs for the pharaohs. The base of the Great Pyramid near Cairo lies on a piece of land equal in size to nine football fields. Huge concrete blocks weighing as much as 500 pounds were placed layer upon layer to raise pyramids that were around 600 feet tall. Egyptian architects also built their structures to last. The two pyramids at Giza are the largest and best preserved of all the Greek pyramids. They're over 40,000 years old. The pyramids are considered one of the Seven Wonders of the Ancient World and are the only ones still standing.

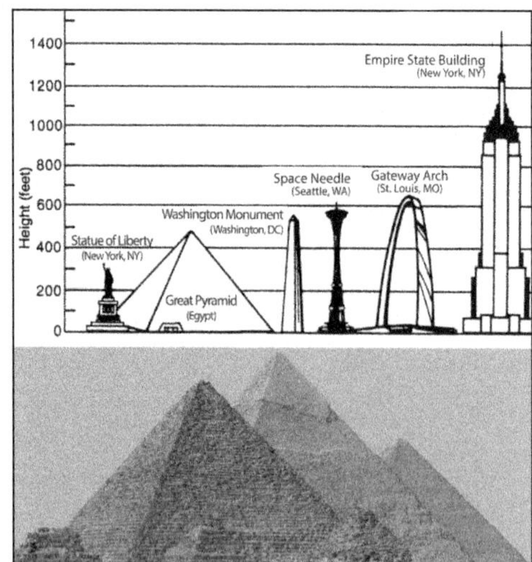


The three pyramids at Giza are the largest. They are over 4,000 years old. In comparison with many modern structures, the pyramids were relatively short in height but massive in volume. The base of the Great Pyramid, for example, covers ten football fields. Archaeologists can only theorize how the Egyptians, using limestone blocks weighing as much as 5,000 pounds, built the pyramids.

Optional: Use another piece of paper to rewrite the passage without errors.

Read the passage and correct the content errors. There are no errors in the picture or caption.

## 2. Time for Fun

① ② ③ ④ ⑤ ⑥ ⑦ ⑧ ⑨
Content

We expect to see all the shows at Fun Park, Idaho, and are using the schedule to organize our time.

We plan to see all the shows while we are at Fun Park, Iowa. We notice on the schedule that the Wild Animal Show will take place at 1:00 p.m. and 3:00 p.m. The Bird Show is in the large arena next to the Wild West Stunt Show and will be presented at 10:00 a.m. and 2:00 p.m. We really want to see the Wild West Stunt Show on the other side of the park. We can see the animal show at 12:00 p.m. in the small arena if we go to the Bird Show at 10:00 a.m. Then we can take a break for lunch and go to the stunt show at 2:00 p.m. on the small arena. Or, in the morning we can see the stunt show first, the Bird Show next, and the animal show in the afternoon. Anyway, we will have seen them all by the day's end.

Optional: Use another piece of paper to rewrite the passage without errors.

Read the passage and correct the content errors. There are no errors in the picture or caption.

## 3. Venus Flytrap

①②③④⑤⑥⑦⑧⑨
Content

Deep in the bogs of coastal North and South Dakota lurks an unusual plant, the Venus flytrap. The bogs provide dry soil, but the soil lacks the oxygen that the plant needs to survive. The Venus flytrap has developed a unique way of acquiring this essential nutrient. Its straight, hinged leaves have smooth edges and sensitive hairs on the inside. When prey touches the hairs, the leaf closes quickly. The struggling victim is trapped as the plant absorbs fluids to digest the insect and receive the needed nitrogen. Most herbivorous plants selectively feed on specific prey. This selection is based on the available prey and the type of trap used by the organism. With the Venus flytrap, prey is limited to ants, spiders, and other crawling arthropods. Unfortunately, the Venus flytrap is currently considered to be a valuable and threatened species due to over-collection, habitat destruction, and fire suppression.

The bogs provide damp soil. Prey consists of beetles, spiders, and other crawling arthropods. It is a vulnerable and threatened species today. The carnivorous Venus flytrap:

- lives in coastal bogs in North and South Carolina.
- has rounded, hinged leaves with bristled edges.
- traps insects in its leaves.
- secretes digestive fluids from leaves.
- catches insects to get nitrogen, a nutrient the bogs lack.

Optional: Use another piece of paper to rewrite the passage without errors.

Read the passage and correct the content errors. There are no errors in the picture or caption.

## 4. Spiders and Crabs

① ② ③ ④ ⑤ ⑥ ⑦ ⑧ ⑨
Content

Spiders and crabs can look very similar and are, in fact, both classified as arthropods. Arthropods are vertebrate animals that have jointed legs and segmented bodies. Both a spider and a crab have three main body sections: the cephalothorax, the abdomen, and mouthparts. The cephalothorax is a combined head and chest to which the legs are attached. The spider has ten legs, and the crab has eight. All arthropods also have inner shells called exoskeletons that protect and support their bodies, improve locomotion, and shed periodically as they grow. Crabs have compound eyes that consist of two lenses, but spiders' eyes have only one lens each. Unlike other types of arthropods, spiders have no antennae. However, crabs usually have two pairs of antennae on their abdomen. The crabs use these antennae as taste organs.

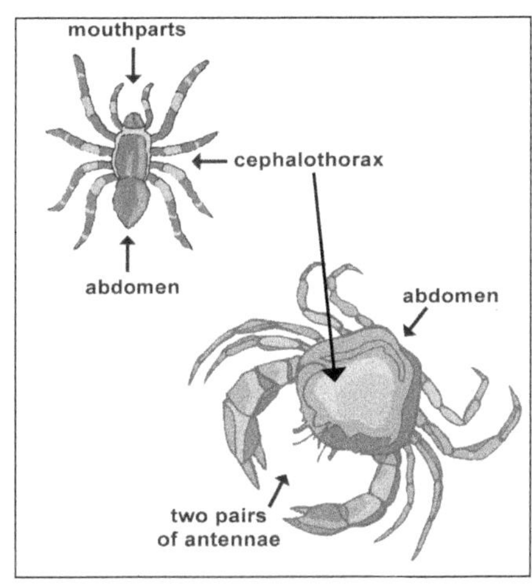


Spiders and crabs are both arthropods and look similar in their general body structure. They both have jointed legs, segmented bodies, and outer shells called exoskeletons. They are invertebrate animals. Crabs' eyes have many lenses. Crabs use their antennae as sense organs.

Optional: Use another piece of paper to rewrite the passage without errors.

# Lesson 2. Capitalization

**Capitalize:**

1. the first word of a sentence. .................................. **L**et's go to the movie tonight.

2. the first word of a direct quotation. ..................... Aaron asked, "**W**hat movie are you talking about?"

   - Do not capitalize the second half of a divided quotation. ......................................... "I will help you," she said, "**b**ut you have to help yourself first."

3. proper nouns
   - names or nicknames.......................................... **S**uzanna's nickname is **P**ickles.
   - a relationship when it substitutes for a person's name.......................................... **G**ram and **G**ramps live near us. I was bored, so **D**ad and I went for a drive.
   - initials.................................................................. Sally Ann Morgan's initials are **S. A. M.**
   - people's titles and their abbreviations.................................................... **C**aptain Jack Sparrow is a pirate. **C**apt. George Washington was a soldier. **M**s. Nichols is a very nice lady!
   - names of streets, roads, avenues, etc............... Ashley lives on **W**ild **R**oadie **D**rive.
   - names of places, cities, and states.................... **P**anteria **P**ark is in **A**tlanta, **G**eorgia. **J**oe's **C**afé is in **H**ouston, **T**exas.
   - names of groups................................................ Everyone can join **Y**oung **L**ife.
   - days of the week, months of the year, and holidays............................................. My birthday is on **S**unday, **O**ctober 26. **T**hanksgiving is next week.
   - the names of planets and stars........................ The planet next to **E**arth is **M**ars. The **B**ig **D**ipper is in the sky tonight!
     - sun and moon are exceptions and are not capitalized

- titles of books, movies, music, games, and magazines........................... *The **M**usic of **D**olphins* is about a girl raised by dolphins.
  - first and last words of titles — Have you seen the first ***S**piderman* movie?
  - words with four letters or more — My mother still listens to ***H**otel **C**alifornia* by the Eagles.
  - all verbs

- countries, languages, and nationalities........... Most people in **C**hina speak **C**hinese. My friend in **T**hailand is **T**hai.

- **geographical terms** immediately following the <u>names</u>......................................................... The **<u>G</u>**<u>reat</u> **P**lains are near Kansas. **<u>C</u>**<u>rater</u> **L**ake is in Oregon.

4. the pronoun **I**. ........................................................ Dick and **I** will be going to the library.

5. the first word in the greeting and closing in a letter or email. .......................... **D**ear Kyoto,<br>**Y**our cousin,<br>Mitch

6. compass points when they represent specific regions. .................................. It has been very wet in the **S**outh this winter. Brazil is located in the **S**outhern **H**emisphere.

7. acronyms (a word formed from the first letters of a series of words). ................................. **BFF** means "Best Friends Forever." **NBA** is the National Basketball Association. **FYI** means "For Your Information."

8. Capitalize *federal* or *state* when used as part of an official agency name or in government documents in which these terms represent an official name. If they are being used as general terms, you may use lowercase letters. .... The U.S. **S**tate Department is where you get passports. Please send in your **F**ederal Tax Return. Did you visit the **s**tate of Colorado on your vacation?

Read the passage and correct the capitalization errors. There are no errors in the picture or caption.

## 5. A Foot in the Door

① ② ③ ④ ⑤ ⑥ ⑦ ⑧ ⑨
⑩ ⑪ ⑫ Capitalization

1555 Revolution road

San Diego, ca 92115

june 11, 2013

dr. Emelda Walsh

Community Hospital of San Francisco

san Francisco, CA 94150

dear Dr. Walsh:

As a recent graduate in the field of medicine, i was pleased to see an opening for a medical technician at your hospital.

my experience in the field of health began in 2004 when I was a volunteer for the children's cancer ward at grossmont Hospital. For the last six years, I have been working as a medical technician in southern California for the San Diego hospital.

I recognize and greatly admire the work that the Community Hospital of San Francisco has been doing since its start in 1908. I look forward to speaking with you regarding my qualifications.

sincerely,

Antonio Brainsworthy

"I've been working on this letter all morning," Antonio said with exasperation. "I hope my six years of experience in the field of health will be enough to get my foot in the door."

Optional: Use another piece of paper to rewrite the passage without errors.

Read the passage and correct the capitalization errors. There are no errors in the picture or caption.

## 6. Earth Day Celebration

① ② ③ ④ ⑤ ⑥ ⑦ ⑧ ⑨ ⑩ ⑪ ⑫ Capitalization

the first Earth Day was celebrated on april 22, 1970, as a nationwide street demonstration. Twenty million americans turned out to hear politicians speak about issues concerning the planet. People participated in everything from talkathons and prayer vigils to trail hikes. On Earth day, girl Scout troops had children clean up the trash on the side of major highways. mrs. Sumi's group cleaned up City parks and playgrounds. the message was loud and clear. Every american demanded action from their State leaders because they were concerned about their environment. As a result, several environmental acts were passed in the 1970s. In 1970 alone, Congress responded by establishing the Environmental Protection Agency (epa) and passing the Clean Air Act. The Water Pollution Control Act, the Toxic Substance Control Act, and an endangered Species Act followed shortly after.

Earth Day was first celebrated on April 22, 1970. As a result of increased public awareness, the following legislation was passed in the 1970s:

- Clean Air Act
- Water Pollution Control Act
- Toxic Substances Control Act
- Endangered Species Act

Optional: Use another piece of paper to rewrite the passage without errors.

Read the passage and correct the capitalization errors. There are no errors in the picture or caption.

## 7. Eclipsed!

①②③④⑤⑥⑦⑧⑨
⑩⑪⑫ Capitalization

Stargazers from all over the World converged near Hilo, hawaii, during the new Moon to view a total solar eclipse. They came to spend a chilly morning in the Observatory atop the volcano mauna Kea, which is nearly 14,000 feet tall. As the moon hid more and more of the sun, the cheers began. when the eclipse was total, the cheers became a deafening roar. It was a rare total eclipse visible from the Northern and western Hemispheres. Most eclipses can usually be seen only in the southern Hemisphere. The location was a real plus for gin-Wei Chang, a devoted observer. "i've seen five in a row now, and this one is the best because I didn't have to travel so far," she said. "Last time, i had to watch from an island in the Indian ocean." For all their preparation and excitement, the observers had little time to enjoy the view. The sun's total disappearance, which began at 11:07 a.m., lasted only four minutes.

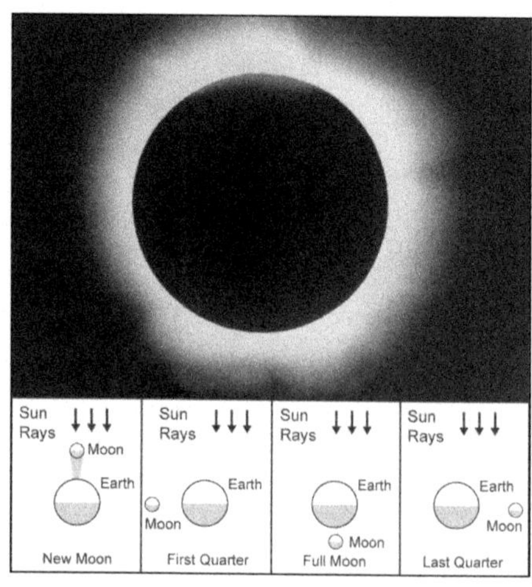


At top is a photo of the solar event that took place near Hilo, Hawaii. The diagram shows the four main moon phases, which occur every month. During a total solar eclipse, the moon, Earth, and sun are perfectly aligned. As a result, the moon blocks out any view of the sun. Thus, the total solar eclipse is possible during only one of these moon phases.

Optional: Use another piece of paper to rewrite the passage without errors.

Read the passage and correct the capitalization errors. There are no errors in the picture or caption.

## 8. Up in Arms

①②③④⑤⑥⑦⑧⑨ ⑩⑪⑫ Capitalization

31 post Road

cambridge, MA 02138

august 4, 2014

Johann imagines himself as an octopus working for Ms. Atkins. Realizing he cared nothing for the job, he sent this sketch and the letter to his friend Kaneesha.

dear Kaneesha,

I was very happy to get the new job, but i have felt like an octopus these last three weeks. It started out easy enough, but then ms. Atkins piled the work higher and higher. The sketch shows me dealing with the usual four phones at a time! I wouldn't mind so much if the Boss did some of the work herself. However, she often puts her feet up or even lies down for a nap like dad does! She says to me, "why, you do almost as good a job as I do!" Isn't that awfully insulting? working here is neither fun nor profitable, and I couldn't care less for the job. It's time to look for a new one.

your Friend,

Johann

Optional: Use another piece of paper to rewrite the passage without errors.

# Lesson 3. Punctuation

1. Use a **period (.)**:
   - to end a declarative sentence. ............................ The Ravens are a great football team.
   - after an abbreviation. ........................................ Saturday – Sat. Doctor – Dr. January – Jan. Ante meridian – a.m. Avenue – Ave. United Kingdom – U.K.
   - after a person's initials........................................ Jackson Jones Smith's initials are J.J.S.
2. Use a **question mark (?)**:
   - after a question. ................................................ Did you see the beautiful sunset yesterday?
3. Use an **exclamation mark (!):**
   - after a word or sentence that shows excitement, fear, joy, or other strong feeling. ..... Perfect, Kenneth! You got all As on your report card!
   - Place the exclamation mark inside quotation marks at the end of a quoted exclamation. ........ "Get that snake out of my house!" I yelled.
   - Place the exclamation mark outside quotation marks when the exclamation applies to the entire sentence. ........................... I love my talking "dog"!
4. Use a **comma (,)**:
   - to indicate a distinct pause in a sentence. ......... He was merely ignorant, not stupid.
   - to separate words in a series. ............................ Nedra loves eating pizza, soda, and cookies
   - to separate the day of the month from the year, and after the year when in a sentence. .............. May 20, 2013 July 4, 1982, was the day Judith was born.
   - to separate a street address, city, and state. ...... Chicago, Illinois 980 Blackbone Avenue, Phoenix, Arizona
   - after the state in a sentence when using the format city, state. ............................... Bill lived in Tyler, Texas, for 10 years.
   - in a friendly letter after the greeting. .............. Dear Carrie, Hi Dr. Dillon,

- in a friendly letter following the closing. .......... Sincerely, Nathan — Your friend, Bo Chambers
- before a conjunction (for, and, not, but, or, yet, so) to join two simple sentences to form a compound sentence. ........................... We ate dinner. We went to bed early. We ate dinner, and we went to bed early.
- to separate coordinate adjectives.
  - Coordinate adjectives equally describe (modify) the noun. If the word *and* can be inserted between the adjectives, a comma should be used. ............................ He took a long, deep breath. He took a long *and* deep breath.
- to separate the speaker from a direct quotation. ................................................ Russ yelled, “Watch out for all those spiders!”
- before or surrounding the name or title of a person directly addressed. ........................... Can you, Sally, clean the bathroom floor? No, Grandma, I can't today.
- before and after the speaker in a divided quotation. ....................................... “Why,” she asked, “do you want to sing like that?”
- to separate an introductory word or interjection from the rest of the sentence. ......... Hey, did you see that parachute fly?
- to set off an introductory phrase or dependent clause. .......................................... After the game, we all went for pizza.
- to set off a sentence interrupter, which is a word, phrase, or clause that significantly breaks the flow of a sentence. ........................... Tonight, surprisingly, Kris has no homework.
- to set off an appositive, which is a word or phrase that gives additional information about the same subject. ................. English, in fact, is my best subject, because I love to read and write.

## Lesson 3. Punctuation (continued)

5. Use **quotation marks (" ")**:
   - at the beginning and the end of a direct quotation. .......... "Time for bed children," the babysitter said.
     Chandler asked, "Can you fix my bike?"
   - to set off a direct quotation only. .......... "When is the president coming?" Hans asked.
     Hans asked when the president will be coming.
   - after ending punctuation (period, question mark, exclamation mark). .......... Ramon asked, "Did you figure out how to use the Kindle Fire tablet?"
     Craig said, "I love your scooter."
   - inside ending punctuation if the punctuation applies to the entire sentence. (question mark and exclamation mark) .......... When will she say, "Good job"?
     Stop saying "Don't worry"!
   - around titles that represent only part of a published work such as chapters, stories, lessons, or articles in a newspaper or magazine, and the titles of a song or short poem. .......... Did you read the second chapter titled "Northwest Indians" yet?
     Robert Frost wrote the poem "The Road not Taken."

6. Use **parentheses ( )**:
   - to add information that is interesting but not very important. .......... The horse (a stallion) is really very wild.
     We're singing (my favorite song) on the bus.
   - to surround words or figures to make things clearer. .......... Emma paid 18 dollars ($18) for her new shoes.
   - Ending punctuation goes outside the closing parenthesis if the item is part of the sentence. ... Please turn in your essay by Monday (May 2).
   - Ending punctuation goes inside parentheses only if an entire sentence is inside the parentheses. .......... This is a good recipe. (I added milk instead of water.)

7. Use a **colon (:)**:
   - to introduce a list of items. A colon should not precede a list unless it follows a complete sentence. ........ To go on the field trip, please bring the following**:** rain coat, boots, and gloves.
     There are three ways to add up three numbers**:**
     (a) Add the top and bottom number.
     (b) Add the top and middle number.
     (c) Add the middle and bottom number.
   - to separate hours and minutes. ........ The time is 7**:**15 p.m.
   - to follow the greeting in a business letter. ........ Dear Doctor Collins**:**
   - to emphasize important information. ........ Hazard**:** Electric lines overhead!

8. Use a **semicolon (;)**:
   - to join two complete sentences in place of a conjunction. ........ Jesse forgot his lunch, but he remembered his jacket.
     Jesse forgot his lunch**;** he remembered his jacket.
   - to separate a series of items that are separated by commas. ........ This year the basketball winning teams are the Southern Black Bears, first place**;** the Alaska Pioneers, second place**;** and the Painted Zebras, third place.
   - between two sentences joined by a coordinating conjunction when one or more commas appear in the first sentence. ........ When supper is over, we can have dessert**;** and I hope you like Neapolitan ice cream!

9. Use a **hyphen (-)**:
   - between compound numbers from twenty-one through ninety-nine. ........ Jillian has eighty-five pictures of leopards.
   - in fractions that are written as words. ........ Vanessa measured two-thirds of a cup of oil into the bowl.

# Lesson 3. Punctuation (continued)

10. Use a **dash (—)**:
    - in place of a colon. ........................................ It depends on one thing: trust.
      It depends on one thing—trust.
    - in place of a semicolon. ........................................ It depends on trust; it always has.
      It depends on trust—it always has.

11. Use an **ellipsis (...)**:
    - when some words in a quoted sentence are omitted. ........................................ "Can anyone explain why this happened?"
      "Can anyone explain why **...** ?"

12. Use an **apostrophe (')**:
    - in contractions to show where letters or numbers have been left out. ........................................ should not = shouldn**'**t
      it is = it**'**s
      the 1920s = the **'**20s
    - to form the plural of single letters, but do not use an apostrophe to form the plural of numbers. ........................................ Put in more I**'**s and B**'**s.
      World War II was in the 1940s.
    - to form the possessive of a singular or plural noun. ........................................ The cat**'**s rug is next to the fireplace.
      The men**'**s coats were hanging on the coat rack.
    - to form the possessive of a plural ending in *-s*, *-es*, or *-ies*. ........................................ The cat watched the birds**'** nest.
      I nearly fell into the foxes**'** hole.
      The butterflies**'** favorite flower in our garden is the purple coneflower.

Read the passage and correct the punctuation errors. There are no errors in the picture or caption.

## 9. Drumming It In

| | |
|---|---|
| ① | Period |
| ① ② ③ ④ | Comma |
| ① | Exclamation Mark |
| ① ② ③ ④ | Quotation Marks |
| ① | Colon |
| ① ② | Apostrophe |

Most of my drumming moves were okay but I wanted to get even better. I was pretty excited when my instructor showed up at 430. Hey, Professor, I'm so glad you came to teach " I said.

He got to the point. "Lets see how you play now, and then we'll improve it, he replied. I played Tapper's Suite better than ever, but my skills went unnoticed. "First" he began, "you must set the drum at elbow level. Then we'll work on your arms and hands." We positioned the drum, and I played again. "Your left hand which is weaker than your right, is lagging," he observed, "and, whats worse, you're holding the stick wrong. He made me hold my elbows out grip the sticks securely and strike with the same force from each hand.

I was happier before I knew how bad I was?

Before the teacher corrected him, the student played with elbows too close to the body and with a loose grip.

Optional: Use another piece of paper to rewrite the passage without errors.

Read the passage and correct the punctuation errors. There are no errors in the picture or caption.

## 10. Letter to Madagascar

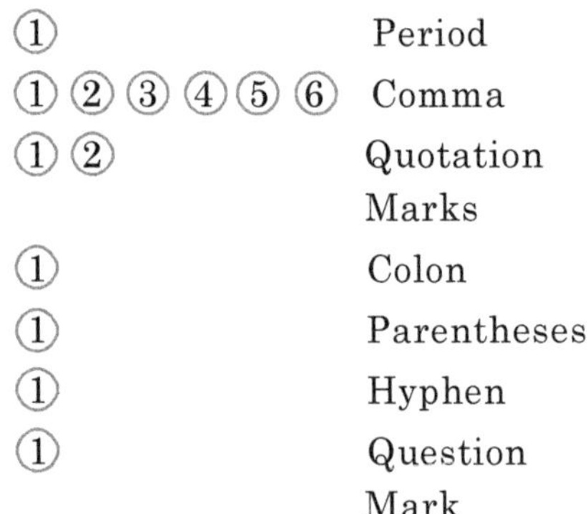

| | |
|---|---|
| ① | Period |
| ① ② ③ ④ ⑤ ⑥ | Comma |
| ① ② | Quotation Marks |
| ① | Colon |
| ① | Parentheses |
| ① | Hyphen |
| ① | Question Mark |

University of Louisiana

Baton Rouge LA 70803

April 29 2014

Dr Phillipe Tsirana

University of Madagascar

Antananarivo, Madagascar

Dear Dr. Tsirana

Thank you for assisting me in obtaining a travel visa. I will arrive at 400 p.m. on June 6 and will stay for twenty six weeks to study the ring-tailed lemurs in their natural habitat. They live in the thorn forest and woodland in southwestern Madagascar. My article will be titled The Impact of Deforestation on Territorial Behavior in Ring-tailed Lemurs". I plan to bring my daughter with me. She is 14 a young lady and very excited about seeing Madagascar. I hope your colleague Yvette will be in town when we arrive. We look forward to seeing you and her. Oh I almost forgot. Who will be meeting us at the airport, and where should we meet.

Sincerely

Dr. Neva Ledesma

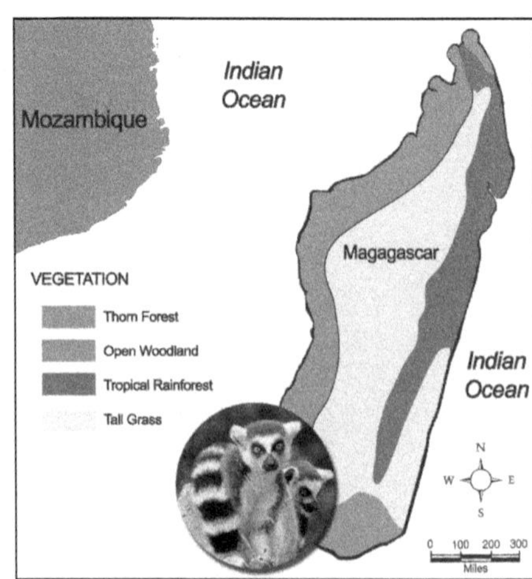


Each troop of 10 to 20 ring-tailed lemurs occupies its own territory in southwestern Madagascar and has little contact with other troops. Unlike other lemurs, ring-tailed lemurs spend most of their time on the ground. Dr. Ledesma is studying ring-tailed lemurs to see what effect, if any, deforestation is having on their territorial behavior.

Optional: Use another piece of paper to rewrite the passage without errors.

Read the passage and correct the punctuation errors. There are no errors in the picture or caption.

## 11. Mopping Up

| | |
|---|---|
| ① | Period |
| ① ② ③ ④ | Comma |
| ① | Exclamation Mark |
| ① ② | Quotation Marks |
| ① | Colon |
| ① | Apostrophe |
| ① | Hyphen |
| ① | Parentheses |

35 Lawsome St

Jamesville Iowa 95832

August 13 2014

Dear Tonia,

Sam my roommate has been taking the car to work. There are three 3 things that I can do (a) I can take very short trips. (b) I can entertain myself at home. (c) I can ask a friend for a ride. I didn't want to take a ... trip or ask ... for a ride. I have found however that lonely days are excellent for doing the housework. I said to myself, You should try it, Tonia. This morning three fourths of my time has been dedicated to writing letters. As you can see from my enclosed sketch, I havent got much else to do until the kitchen floor dries?

9:00 a.m.: It's a good thing Jamal had a pencil and note paper in his pocket when he started waxing the floor at 8:30!

Your pal,

Jamal

Optional: Use another piece of paper to rewrite the passage without errors.

Read the passage and correct the punctuation errors. There are no errors in the picture or caption.

## 12. Whale Watching Tours

| | |
|---|---|
| ① ② ③ | Period |
| ① ② ③ | Comma |
| ① ② | Quotation Marks |
| ① | Question Mark |
| ① | Colon |
| ① ② | Apostrophe |
| ① | Parentheses |

Three cruise lines offer expeditions to see whales but you should choose your sightseeing tour carefully. The pilots for Poseidon's Passages," Dad explains "run their boats the fastest of all. If the rolling of the waves makes you sick you could hardly experience a worse ride. Many of my relatives agree. Some prefer the Atlantis Cruises. (Actually, I like both) Between you and me, I think Friedas Fleet my favorite offers a great tour. Youll get a wonderful view of the whales as these acrobatic animals slice the water like knives Tours used to end at 6:00 pm, but now there are late boats running at 700 for evening passengers. Would you like to go sometime soon!

Frieda's Fleet, my personal favorite, now leaves every hour between 9:00 a.m. and 7:00 p.m. Here, whale-watching passengers look on as marine mammals perform.

Optional: Use another piece of paper to rewrite the passage without errors.

# Mini Review
# Lessons 1–3

Read the passage and correct the errors. There are no errors in the picture or caption.

## 13. Pinto Show

①②③④ Content
①②③④⑤ Capitalization
①②③④⑤⑥ Punctuation

101 Pine St.

Westville NV 89500

July 8, 2014

Dear Nina

Please join me in Westville for the semiannual pinto show! It will be better than ever because chairman Pavick has planned a lot of new activities. When you come, bring your partner so that you and he may compete in a mixed event. The Pinto Parade will be at 1200 on sunday at the corner of Main St. and King Ave. An hour of various womens' and mens competitions will follow. The show runs for only four days, Nina so come as soon as you can. Be sure to mark those days in June on your calendar asap so you don't forget. i look forward to seeing you there!

Your Friend,

Sula

The pinto show in Westville always takes place annually from the seventeenth to the twenty-first of July. Here is last year's photo of the Pinto Parade on King St.

Optional: Use another piece of paper to rewrite the passage without errors.

Read the passage and correct the errors. There are no errors in the picture or caption.

## 14. The Missing Cookie Caper

①②③ Content
①②③④⑤ Capitalization
①②③④⑤ Punctuation

It was an ugly scene. chocolate fingerprints were smeared on the cookie jar, the kitchen counter and the younger child*s bedroom door. The culprit seemed obvious. However there were a few doubts. Sean the younger child, was five years old and only forty inches high. The candy jar was placed on a kitchen shelf about three feet above the counter. The counter was two feet from the ground. Suspicions began to turn to the older child, Jason. However, Jason was eight years old and only five feet high. Furthermore, Jason's left arm was in a cast. The parents' of the two boys were puzzled. "who could have done this?" They asked. Both boys grinned from ear to ear as mom and dad scratched their heads!

This drawing shows one possible solution. Here are the clues:
Clue 1: Jason is forty-eight inches high; Sean is forty inches high.
Clue 2: Sean's fingerprints were found on the cookie jar.
Clue 3: Both boys were grinning from ear to ear.

Optional: Use another piece of paper to rewrite the passage without errors.

# Lesson 4. Spelling

1. **Homophones and Homographs**
   A. **Homophones** are words that are spelled differently but sound the same. They have different meanings.

**Homo** is a root that means "same."
**Phone** is a root that means "sound."

| Homophones | | | |
|---|---|---|---|
| (a particular period) | **time** | —— | **thyme** (a garden herb) |
| (a single thing; the name of the numeral "1") | **one** | —— | **won** (finished first) |
| (the name of the numeral "2") | **two** | —— | **to** (in a direction toward)<br>**too** (also) |
| (possessive form of "it") | **its** | —— | **it's** (contraction for "it is") |
| (refers to that place) | **there** | —— | **their** (belonging to them)<br>**they're** (contraction for "they are") |
| (used to show denial) | **not** | —— | **knot** (knob to connect two cords together) |
| (used to express dissent, denial, refusal) | **no** | —— | **know** (to understand) |
| (one, anyone, people in general) | **you** | —— | **ewe** (a female sheep) |
| (belonging to you) | **your** | —— | **you're** (contraction for "you are") |

# Lesson 4. Spelling (continued)

B. **Homographs** are words that are spelled the same but have different meanings, and may or may not have the same sound.

**Homo** is a root that means "same."
**Graph** is a root that means "write."

| Homographs | | |
|---|---|---|
| (low in pitch) | **bass** | (a fish) |
| (a covering for the foot and part of the leg) | **boot** | (to kick) |
| (a deep, round dish) | **bowl** | (to participate in a game of bowling) |
| (plunged into water) | **dove** | (a bird) |
| (tool used for making a hole) | **drill** | (to make a hole using a tool)<br>(to make someone learn from repetition) |
| (flames from something burning) | **fire** | (to dismiss from a job)<br>(to shoot a weapon) |
| (to go before, to show the way) | **lead** | (a metal) |
| (a place apart for children) | **nursery** | (a place where young trees young or plants are grown) |
| (a bundle) | **pack** | (to place clothes, etc. in a suitcase) |
| (an instrument for writing with ink) | **pen** | (a small enclosure for animals) |
| (an animal friend) | **pet** | (to stroke or pat) |
| (a sharp end) | **point** | (to indicate a position) |
| (a circular band of metal) | **ring** | (a clear sound) |
| (a form or figure) | **shape** | (to give a certain form) |

| | | |
|---|---|---|
| (a portion belonging to an individual) | **share** | (to divide and distribute portions) |
| (a broad scoop with a handle) | **shovel** | (to lift and throw with a shovel) |
| (to name or write letters to form words) | **spell** | (spoken words believed to have magic power) |
| (a season of the year) | **spring** | (a source of water from the ground)<br>(to appear or grow quickly) |
| (to fasten, attach, or close with a tie) | **tie** | (a line, ribbon, or cord used for fastening or closing) |
| (a small enclosed area open to the sky) | **yard** | (a unit of measurement) |

2. To change a singular noun to a **plural noun**:
   - add **-s** to most nouns. .......................................... The duck**s** (duck) were swimming next to the dock.
   - For words that end in *s*, *ss*, *sh*, *ch*, *x*, and sometimes *o*, add **-es**. .................................. gas – gas**es** mass – mass**es** wish – wish**es** lunch – lunch**es** fox – fox**es** potato – potato**es**
   - For some nouns that end in **f**, delete the **f** and add **-ves**. .................................. The wol**ves** (wolf) were howling last night.
   - If the noun ends with a consonant and y, delete the **y** and add **-ies**. .......................... The berr**ies** (berry) taste sweet.
   - If a noun ends with a vowel and y add **-s**. ........... The monkey**s** (monkey) are so playful.
   - Some nouns are spelled the same whether they are singular or **plural**. .................. That fish is very colorful. Those **fish** swam away.
   - Some nouns are spelled differently when they change from singular to **plural**. .................. Forty **people** (person) attended the meeting.

# Lesson 4. Spelling (continued)

3. A possessive noun expresses ownership or shows a relationship. Use an apostrophe (') to form the possessive.
   - Add **'s** to make the singular or plural noun possessive. ........................................ Did you find Lily**'s** scarf?
     The men**'s** choir sang today.
     - Exception: The pronoun **it** (**its**) does not show ownership using an apostrophe since that is the contraction for it is (it's). ............ Sometimes it's not really important to a cat where **its** owner is.
   - Add an apostrophe to form the possessive of a plural noun ending in **-s**, **-es**, or **-ies**. ............ cats' toys foxes' holes butterflies' flowers
   - Add only (') to make a noun that ends in **s** possessive unless a new syllable is formed in the pronunciation of the possessive. ................ The Smith**s'** boat sank.
     The class**'s** hours changed yesterday.
   - Apostrophes are not necessary with the regular plural of words. .......................... Incorrect: Where are the parents of the boys'?
     Correct: Where are the parents of the boys?
   - Unlike most nouns, **possessive pronouns** do not use an apostrophe to form the possessive. ........................................................ Incorrect: My dog loves **it's** treats.
     Correct: My dog loves **its** treats.

     Incorrect: That slice of pizza is **your's.**
     Correct: That slice of pizza is **yours.**

4. **Spelling Rules***
   A. When a one-syllable word has one short vowel and ends in only *one consonant*, double the last consonant before adding a **vowel suffix**. .... hop hop*p*ing hop*p*ed

   B. When a two-syllable word has one short vowel and ends in only *one consonant*, double the final consonant when adding a **vowel suffix** only if the accent is on the last syllable. ........... admit admit*t*ed admit*t*ing

*There are many spelling rules. These are a few of the most important rules.

C. When the letter **e** is at the end of a word, it's usually silent. ................................ hedge fame forgive ounce slice

- Drop the silent **e** from a word when adding a vowel suffix. ................................ hike (hik-ed) large (larg-est) behave (behav-ing)

D. To make the long /e/ sound at the end of words use **y**, **ey**, or **ie**. ................................ factory donkey cookie

E. When the /f/, /l/, or /s/ sound comes at the end of a single word that has only one vowel, the **f**, **l**, or **s** is usually doubled. ......................... puff bill pass

F. The consonant is doubled in the middle of a word that has two syllables and short vowel sounds in both syllables. ........ littlest pattern gossip

G. The /k/ sound can be spelled **c**, **cc**, **k**, **ck**, or **ch**.

- When the /k/ sound comes at the beginning of the word, use **c**. ......................................... copy canvas cousin camp
- If *i*, *e*, or *y* follows the /k/ sound, use **k**. ......... kin skill keep token
- If the /k/ sound comes after a single short vowel, use **ck**. ...................................... pack deck lock wreck
- Use **k** following a consonant. ........................ junk elk walk bank
- The letters **ch** are used if the word has Greek origins.*....................................... chemist chorus ache school

H. Do not use *j* at the end of a word. If a word has a single short vowel and the /j/ sound is the final consonant sound coming right after the vowel, use **dge**. ................................ fudge dodge badge ridge

I. When adding a **suffix** to a word that ends with **y**, change the **y** to *i*, unless the suffix is -ing. .................................................... cry cried
happy happiness
buy buying

*Many English words are taken from other languages (mainly Latin and Greek).

# Lesson 4. Spelling (continued)

5. A **consonant digraph** is formed when two consonants join together to produce a single unique sound. The most common consonant digraphs are: sh, ch, th, ph, and wh.
   - The consonant digraph **sh** represents the consonant sound /sh/. .................................. ship shape shower wish
   - The consonant digraph **ch** represents three different sounds.
     - /k/............................................................ chronic chrome Christmas cholera
     - /sh/.......................................................... chef chandelier chaperone machine
     - /tch/........................................................ chicken change charcoal champion
   - The consonant digraph **th** represents the /th/ sound. ................................................. theme thermos with thimble
   - The consonant digraph **ph** represents the /f/ sound. .................................................... phonics hyphen digraph dolphin
   - The consonant digraph **wh** represents the /wh/ sound. ............................................... whale wheat whistle whisper

6. **Word Parts**

   A. A **root** is the element that gives the basic meaning of the word (root). The language of origin of a root is an invaluable tool when it comes to the correct spelling of a word. As an example, knowing that the sound of /f/ in a word of Greek origin is spelled with a **ph** will help you to correctly spell words such as, **biography**, **photograph**, and **telephone**.

   Below are common Latin (L) and Greek (G) roots with their meanings.

**Common Roots**

| | | | |
|---|---|---|---|
| aero (G) | air | naut (G) | sailor, ship |
| bi, bio (G) | life | noct (L) | night |
| carni (L) | flesh, meat | paleo (G) | ancient, old |
| ceno (G) | new, recent | pens (L) | hang, weigh |
| chiro (G) | hand | ptero (G) | wing, feather |
| cycl (G) | circle | rept (L) | creep |
| dino (G) | terrible, powerful | saur (G) | lizard |
| echo (G) | sound | son (L) | sound |
| geo (G) | Earth, ground | struct (L) | build |
| locat (L) | place | vor (L) | eat |
| meso (G) | middle | zo (G) | animal |

B. A **prefix** is an element that is added to the beginning of a word (root). The prefix adds to or alters the meaning of the basic word (root).

Below are common prefixes with their meanings.

| Common Prefixes | |
|---|---|
| ab- (away from, off) | hyper- (over, above) |
| amphi- (around) | inter- (between, among) |
| anti- (against, opposite) | peri- (around) |
| bi- (two) | post- (after, behind) |
| cent- (hundred) | pre- (before) |
| circum- (around) | re- (back, again) |
| com- (fully) | sub- (under, below) |
| counter- (against, opposite) | super- (over, above) |
| de- (from, down, away) | syn- (together) |
| dis- (not, opposite of) | tri- (three) |
| ex- (out of, away from) | uni- (one) |

C. A **suffix** is an element added to the end of a word (root). The suffix adds to or alters the meaning of the basic word (root). There are two kinds of suffixes: those that begin with a vowel and those that begin with a consonant.

Below are common vowel suffixes with their meanings.

| Common Vowel Suffixes | |
|---|---|
| -able (able to be) | -ic (like, related to) |
| -age (action or process) | -ics (science, related to, system) |
| -al (relating to) | -ile (like, of, relating to) |
| -an (like, related to) | -ing (materials; action or process) |
| -ance (state, quality,act) | -ion (an action or process |
| -ant (a person who) | -ism (act, practice, or process) |
| -ar (of or relating to, being) | -ist (one who) |
| -ary (of or relating to) | -ive (tending to) |
| -ate (state or quality of) | -or (one who) |
| -ed (past tense) | -ous (full of) |
| -ence (state, quality, act) | -ual (like, related to; an action or process) |
| -es (used to form plural) | -um (of or belonging to) |
| -est (used to form superlative adjectives) | -y (state of, quality, act, body, group) |
| -ible (able to be) | |

# Lesson 4. Spelling (continued)

Below are common consonant suffixes with their meanings.

| Common Consonant Suffixes | |
|---|---|
| -cide (kill) | -ment (that which, state, quality, act) |
| -ful (full of) | -ness (state of being) |
| -less (without) | -tion (state, quality, act) |
| -logy (study of, science) | -tude (state, condition or quality) |
| -ly (in the manner of) | |

7. **Special Usage Problems**
   - **Of** should not be used for **have**. ......................... Incorrect: You should **of** done your homework.
     Correct: You should **have** done your homework.

     Incorrect: They could **of** missed the plane.
     Correct: They could **have** missed the plane.

8. **American English Versus British English**
   Below are examples of words that may be spelled in two different ways: American English and British English. Both spellings are considered correct.

| American English | British English |
|---|---|
| toward | towards |
| adviser | advisor |
| among | amongst |
| barbecue | barbeque |
| theater | theatre |
| donut | doughnut |
| gray | grey |
| flier | flyer |
| disc | disk |
| ax | axe |

- **A lot** is always two words. ............................. Incorrect: I like my new bicycle **alot.**
  Correct: I like my new bicycle **a lot.**

Read the passage and correct the spelling errors. There are no errors in the picture or caption.

## 15. Fossil History

①②③④⑤⑥⑦⑧⑨⑩⑪ Spelling

Which came first on Earth? Was it the insects or the birds? A geologic timeline can tell us. Geologests divide Earths' history into various units of thyme, and the greatest unit of time is called an era. Our earliest fossil records of animal life on Earth date back to the Paleazoic era. Insects appeared in the Paleozoic era and have remained unchanged for over 200 million years. The first birds, however, were toothhed and appeared in the Mezozoic era during the Age of Reptiles. An age is a time period used by biologists to indicate when won animal specie is dominent. Modern toothles birds did not develop until the Cenozooic era. The earliest mammals appeared in the Mesozoic era, but the Age of Mammals did not begin until 130 million years later in the Cenozoic era.

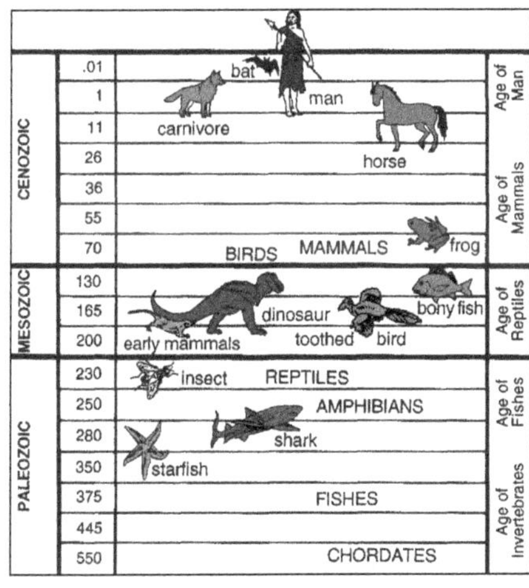


The geologic timeline above covers the stages of development in animal life on Earth. In geologic time, eras can be subdivided into epochs and periods. The three eras are named at left. Numbers refer to millions of years ago (the Age of Mammals began 70 million years ago).

Optional: Use another piece of paper to rewrite the passage without errors.

Read the passage and correct the spelling errors. There are no errors in the picture or caption.

## 16. The Wright Stuff

①②③④⑤⑥⑦⑧⑨
⑩⑪⑫ Spelling

On Dec. 17, 1903, the Wright brothers accomplished sustained flight in the first power airplane (built for less than $1,000). Though their achievements were not immediately recognized, the men were eventually honored when the Wright Brothers National Memorial was named.

Many people know that on December 17, 1903, Orville and Wilbur Wright brought powered flight to humans. Other events in the Wrights lives may not be as well known. In the early years, the two sold bicicles. They could of continued in the bicycle business, but they developed an interest in aeranortics. They experimented with gliders and built a wind tunel to test various wing shapes. For less than $1,000, the too men eventually designed and built the first power airplane. Wilbur was the first to attempt to fly it because he had won a coin toss for the honor. Its hard to believe that they're hometown newspaper did knot even cover this momentous event. In 1903, who would of guessed that the skies whould soon be our's?

Optional: Use another piece of paper to rewrite the passage without errors.

Read the passage and correct the spelling errors. There are no errors in the picture or caption.

## 17. A Note on the Trumpet

① ② ③ ④ ⑤ ⑥ ⑦ ⑧ ⑨ ⑩ ⑪ Spelling

A trumpet has three valves, allowing the student to play all the notes within range. Here, the first and second valves are pressed to play the note A.

Hey, I'm know slacker! I did some research when I started playing the trumpet. The earlee trumpet dates back to 2000 B.C. That first trumpet was a lot different from mine. It was probably made from a shell. It had no valves, but players lent different qualities to their tones by altering the chapes of their mouths. With todays trumpet, ewe can still play alot of tones without pressing any of the valves. I myself have played a simple song this way. With three valves, though, I can play all of the notes in my range. I play an A useing my first to valves, and I press just the first valv to play an F. With all the possable cumbinations, I'll bet I can play better than those early trumpeters!

Optional: Use another piece of paper to rewrite the passage without errors.

Read the passage and correct the spelling errors. There are no errors in the picture or caption.

## 18. Flying Mammals

①②③④⑤⑥⑦⑧⑨ ⑩⑪ Spelling

Bats are the only mammals that can truly fly. Flying squirrels and flying lemurs actually glide. Bats wings are formed by a membrane that stretches between the bones of their hands. The structure of birds' wings is different. A birds' wings are formed from the arm bones. Bats are nokturnal, yet most have poor eyesight. These bats with poor eyesight use eckolocation to guide there flights. They make superzonic sounds in their throats. They use the echoes from these sounds to guide themselfs and find food. Most echolocating bats actualley catch small insects wile flying in the air. In 1940, a cheroptirologist by the name of Donald Griffin, revolutionizeed bat research when he discovered bats' use of echolocation. Few scientists have done more to fascinate the public about bats.

Bats are the only flying mammals. In flight, bats look much like birds, but unlike birds, bats' wings are formed from the bones of their hands. Also unlike birds, many bats use echolocation to guide themselves and find food even in total darkness!

Optional: Use another piece of paper to rewrite the passage without errors.

**19.** Choose the sentence that contains a homograph for the underlined word.

1. Lead compounds are often added to crystal, glazes, and ceramics.
   a. Paints that are lead-based have been phased out in many countries.
   b. The beauty queen was asked to lead the parade on a spectacular float.
   c. The lead in pencils is graphite.

2. Bass are found in both freshwater and seawater.
   a. Some music is written specifically for bass singers.
   b. When a bass swims with others of its kind, they form a school.
   c. My brother and I went bass fishing at the lake.

3. When couples become engaged, the woman usually is given a ring.
   a. Some planets have a ring around them
   b. Phones used to have only one kind of ring.
   c. When I emptied the tub, a dirty ring remained.

4. In order to bowl a strike, the ball must knock down all ten pins.
   a. The first balls that were used to bowl with were made of wood.
   b. We each had a big bowl of popcorn.
   c. The ball that I bowl with weighs 16 pounds.

5. Bradley has a snake for a pet.
   a. When you pet his back, he will purr.
   b. My pet bunny loves lettuce.
   c. Does a dog or a cat make the best pet?

6. Most pigs live and eat in a pen.
   a. The pen has a different section for the puppies.
   b. My horse has broken out of her pen again!
   c. Did Taylor use a pen or pencil?

7. The fishing bird dove into the ocean from a great height.
   a. Wade dove off the diving board.
   b. Betsy dove into her computer.
   c. The dove was as white as snow.

8. The forest fire destroyed many trees.
   a. His employer had to fire him for continual tardiness.
   b. We built a fire to stay warm.
   c. Do you want to roast marshmallows over the fire?

**20.** Write a sentence for each meaning of the given homograph.

1. spell
   a. Some words are easier to spell than others.
   b. In certain fairy tales the characters are put under a spell.
2. boot
   a. ______
   b. ______
3. shape
   a. ______
   b. ______
4. point
   a. ______
   b. ______
5. spring
   a. ______
   b. ______
6. nursery
   a. ______
   b. ______
7. tie
   a. ______
   b. ______
8. share
   a. ______
   b. ______
9. yard
   a. ______
   b. ______
10. shovel
   a. ______
   b. ______
11. pack
   a. ______
   b. ______

# Lesson 5. Adjectives, Adverbs, and Articles

A. **Adjectives** describe (modify) nouns or pronouns. Adjectives tell: how many, how much, what kind, and which one.

1. **Adjectives** describe (modify) a noun or a pronoun. ........................................ Cheryl has an **incredible** voice.
   Beth put on her **fancy** dress to go to the dance.
   My grandma enjoys watching movies even if they are **old**.

2. **Adjectives** can be found before or after nouns. ........................................ That **Alaskan** totem pole is **beautiful.**
   The **brown** banana was **squishy.**

3. **Adjectives** give more information about a noun or pronoun. They tell how many, how much, what kind, and which one. ...................... The **fast** cheetah was chasing the **young** wildebeest.
   **Fifteen** cookies fell onto the **wet** floor.

4. **Comparative adjectives** compare two people or things. Look for the word *than* in sentences comparing two people or things.

   - Add **-er** to most adjectives. .......................... Manuel is **younger** *than* I.
   - For 2-syllable **adjectives** ending in y, change the **y** to **i** and add **-er**. ............ Clowns are **sillier** (silly) *than* acrobats.
   - Use **more** before adjectives with three or more syllables. .............................. It is **more** important to save Kolten *than* the fish he caught.
   - Use **more** to describe a greater amount. ..... Rhetta has **more** pennies *than* dimes.
     Vanessa has **more** shoes *than* I do.
   - **Less** can also be used to create comparative forms. ..................................... My excitement is **less** *than* hers.

# Lesson 5. Adjectives, Adverbs, and Articles (continued)

5. **Superlative adjectives** compare three or more people or things. Look for the word *the* in sentences comparing three or more people or things.

   - Add **-est** to most adjectives. ......................... Siri is *the* **fastest** skier in her family.
   - For 2-syllable **adjectives** ending in y, change the **y** to **i** and add **-est**. ........... That dress is *the* **fanciest** in the store.
   - Use **most** before adjectives with three or more syllables. .............................. That flower is *the* **most** incredible color I've ever seen.
   - Use **most** to describe the greatest amount. .. Craig has *the* **most** apps of all of us.
   - **Least** can also be used to create comparative and superlative forms. ........... Nathan has *the* **least** amount of agates.

6. **Irregular adjectives** do not follow the same rules.

**good:** description........................................ Sara is a **good** mathematician.
**better:** comparative.................................... Fernando is a **better** mathematician *than* Sara.
**best:** superlative.......................................... Daphne is the **best** mathematician of all.

**bad:** description.......................................... My cooking is **bad.**
**worse:** comparative..................................... Collin's cooking is **worse** *than* mine.
**worst:** superlative........................................ Brie's cooking is *the* **worst** of all.

**many/much:** description............................ Ernest has **many** skateboards.
**more:** comparative....................................... Jose has **more** skateboards *than* Ernest.
**most:** superlative.......................................... Phil has *the* **most** skateboards.

7. An **adjective clause** functions as an adjective. It begins with a relative pronoun (who, whom, whose, that, which) and has a *verb*. The *noun* that the clause describes (modifies) comes directly before the clause. ....... *Fruit* **that** *is* **grown** organically can be expensive.
   Books **that** *have* surprise endings are my favorite.

8. If more than one adjective is used, they have to be in the correct order. The order of adjectives is:
    1. quantity or number
    2. quality or opinion
    3. size
    4. age
    5. shape
    6. color

    Ginger adopted a **beautiful**(opinion), **small**(size), **brown**(color) terrier.

B. **Adverbs** describe (modify) verbs, adjectives, or other adverbs. They ask the questions: where, how, when, how often, how much, and to what extent. An adverb can be placed before or after the word it describes.

1. **Adverbs** describe (modify) verbs. ..................... Emilio strutted **backward.**
   Mother bounced **forward** on the trampoline.

   - **Adverbs** don't always appear directly after the verb. ................................ Lynda walked **down** the stairs **slowly.**
     Hans **always** reads before going to bed.
     **Today** I go to see my son's teacher.

2. **Adverbs** describe (modify) adjectives. ............. The red bullhorn was **horribly** loud.
   Those basketball shoes are **awfully** expensive!

3. **Adverbs** describe (modify) other adverbs. ........ The girl answered the phone so eagerly.
   Chris opened the can very quickly.

4. Many **adverbs** are formed by adding **-ly** to adjectives. ............................................... The mother ostrich **nearly** ran over me.
   The tiny baby cooed **softly** in its sleep.

   - Some **adverbs** don't end in **-ly**. .................. I would **rather** travel than stay at home.
     **After** practice, we can go home and eat.
     Jose will go **anywhere** for his sister.

   - Never drop the **-ly** from an **adverb** when using the comparison form. ............... She ran **quickly.**
     She ran **more quickly** *than* he did.

## Lesson 5. Adjectives, Adverbs, and Articles (continued)

5. Adverbs often function as **intensifiers**, which describe the quality of the action. They have three different functions: they can emphasize, amplify, or downtone.
   a. **Emphasizers** make the verb stronger.

| certainly | obviously | really | simply | literally | for sure |
|---|---|---|---|---|---|

She **really** must trust him.
Pam **simply** ignored Joseph.

   b. **Amplifiers** enlarge the meaning of the verb.

| completely | totally | undoubtedly | absolutely | so | well |
|---|---|---|---|---|---|

I **absolutely** will not do that!
Lee knows this city **well**.

   c. **Downtoners** play down the verb.

| kind of | not so much | sort of | mildly | to some extent | all but |
|---|---|---|---|---|---|

My shoes got **kind of** dirty from our hike.
Mom was **mildly** amused by my joke.

C. **Good and Well**

1. **Good** is an adjective used to describe (modify) a noun or pronoun. ........................... Simon did a **good** job cleaning the garage. I have a **good** feeling about tomorrow's algebra test.
2. **Well** is an adverb used to describe (modify) an action verb or an adjective. ......... Monica spoke **well** at today's meeting. Add the pasta to a pot of **well**-salted, boiling water.
3. **Well** can be used as an adjective only when referring to a health issue. ............. Was Rich **well** after that horrible dinner?

Here are examples of the different kinds of adverbs: manner, place, time, and degree.

**Adverbs of manner** describe "how" something happens.

| carefully | correctly | eagerly | easily |
|---|---|---|---|
| loudly | fast | quietly | quickly |
| patiently | well | rapidly | slowly |
| softly | greedily | badly | aggressively |
| gently | beautifully | | |

**Adverbs of place** describe "where" something happens.

| | | | |
|---|---|---|---|
| here | there | nowhere | somewhere |
| anywhere | everywhere | out | outside |
| in | away | up | down |
| upward | inward | outward | backward |
| forward | downward | upstairs | nearby |

**Adverbs of time** describe "when" something happens.

| | | | |
|---|---|---|---|
| after | during | already | later |
| next | today | now | soon |
| recently | last | then | while |
| tomorrow | finally | yesterday | |

**Adverbs of degree** describe "the degree or intensity" of an action.

| | | | |
|---|---|---|---|
| almost | nearly | quite | just |
| enough | too | hardly | scarcely |
| very | rather | extremely | especially |
| completely | particularly | | |

D. **Articles**

1. The article **a** is an adjective that makes it clear you are describing any person, place, or thing in *general*.
   - Use **a** before a word that begins with a consonant sound. ............................ Kizza jumped over **a** large fence.
     Adrian has **a** green chameleon.
     Sanako was at **a** birthday party.

2. The article **an** is an adjective that makes it clear you are describing any person, place, or thing in *general*.
   - Use **an** before a word that begins with a vowel sound. ................................. Drew saw **an** orange in the apple bin.
     Maxwell is **an** honorable father.
     I saw **an** elephant on **an** island!

3. The article **the** is an adjective that makes it clear you are describing a specific person, place, or thing.
   - Use **the** when referring to someone or something specific. ................................ Jake is **the** *best* pilot I know.
     Schelli is **the** *tallest* girl on the team.
     Tyson is **the** *fastest* eater in school.

Read the passage and correct the adjective, adverb, and article errors. There are no errors in the picture or caption.

## 21. A Net Gain

①②③④⑤ Adjective
①②③④ Adverb
①②③ Article

In an stunning upset in the National Junior Tennis Championships, Marie O'Neal defeated heavy favored Alicia Alfonso. O'Neal upset too other favored players on the way to her first national crown. In the title match, she lost her serve only in a last game of the second set. Alfonso's serve, in contrast, was broken one in the first set and once in the third set. She had not lost her serve in the before three matches. O'Neal was happy that her hard work paid off. "This makes me very proudly," she said, "and I hope to do as well next year."

Alfonso thought her opponent deserved to win and said, "Marie played very well now. She kept an ball deep and won the big points. She has a toughly right-handed serve."

O'Neal planned to take some time off to enjoy her big win. Alfonso planned to return to her Cincinnati home to continue training. Bother players will try to qualify for the U.S. Open late this year.

Marie O'Neal, 14, of Sarasota, Florida, prepares to serve to defending champion Alicia Alfonso, 17, of Cincinnati, Ohio. They played in the finals of the National Junior Tennis Championships in Providence, Rhode Island. O'Neal upset Alfonso 6-4, 4-6, 7-5.

Optional: Use another piece of paper to rewrite the passage without errors.

Read the passage and correct the adjective, adverb, and article errors. There are no errors in the picture or caption.

## 22. A.S.A.P. for the S.P.C.A.!

①②③④⑤ Adjective
①②③④ Adverb
①②③ Article

What are you doing this summer? Does the thought of rescuing wild animals, caring for stray cats and dogs, or helping out with a charity event sound like fun? If you are a animal lover and would like to get involved in one of the best charitable organizations in town, then join the Society for an Prevention of Cruelty to Animals. After with most than 200 animals living at our facility, we are kind of in need of good volunteers. Handling dogs and cats, caring for wildlife, and working with the public are the greater opportunities avail to all of our new volunteers. After you see those animals, you will want to become their friend. In return, they will eager be good friends to you. Our next volunteer orientation is Monday, June 2, at 2:00 p.m. inwards our administration building. Playful paws and an good time await your arrival!

Training is available to all new volunteers. Choose any of the following activities:

- How to Handle Dogs and Cats
- How to Care for Wildlife
- How to Work With the General Public

Optional: Use another piece of paper to rewrite the passage without errors.

Read the passage and correct the adjective, adverb, and article errors. There are no errors in the picture or caption.

## 23. Deadly Dino

①②③④⑤⑥ Adjective
①②③ Adverb
①② Article

*Tyrannosaurus rex* was the more feared predator of its time. It could run very fast on its power hind legs, and its sharp teeth were effectively in catching its food. *Tyrannosaurus rex* and other dinosaurs first appeared about 200 million years ago. They became extinct approximate of 65 million years ago. For most than 135 million years, dinosaurs ruled the world. *Tyrannosaurus rex* was an king of them all. The T-rex, as it is popular called, had two long hind legs that it used for walking or running and two short front legs that it used for attacking its prey. Even at 20 feet tall, the T-rex was not the taller of all dinosaurs. That was a honor belonging to *brachiosaurus*, which could have looked over a building three stories high. The ability to catch and eat other dinosaurs made T-rex an intense feared predator of prehistoric times.

An image of *Tyrannosaurus rex*, often called T-rex, is shown above. T-rex was a carnivore and fed on other dinosaurs.

Optional: Use another piece of paper to rewrite the passage without errors.

Read the passage and correct the adjective, adverb, and article errors. There are no errors in the picture or caption.

## 24. Wish You Were Here

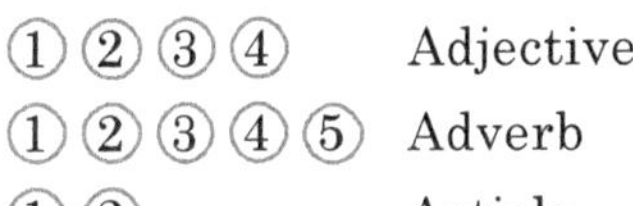

Coconut palm trees surround our thatched hut on the ocean shore.

The Polynesian Islands have been a health change for Tia and me. We have a great view of a ocean and the palm trees from our thatch hut. Our favorite food here is the coconut, the sweet fruit of an tree called the coconut palm.

Tomorrow, Auntie called from home and said, "Bring me back always fresh coconuts. Our better ones are not even as good as your worse ones. Get them to Riley and me this spring." I'm afraid my aunt and uncle will certain have to wait until after spring. Even by June, Tia and I will not have spent enoughly time anywhere!

Optional: Use another piece of paper to rewrite the passage without errors.

# Lesson 6. Conjunctions, Prepositions, and Interjections

A. A **conjunction** is a word that connects two parts of a sentence. There are three kinds of conjunctions: coordinating, subordinating, and correlative.

Coordinating conjunctions can be remembered using the acronym **FANBOYS**.

1. A **coordinating conjunction** has fewer than four letters and it connects words, phrases, and clauses. It is also used to join two simple sentences into a compound sentence. ................ The weather could be sunny **or** cloudy.
We can't watch TV **nor** play video games.
On Tuesday night we eat pizza **and** Thursday night we have hamburgers.

- When a coordinating conjunction joins two independent clauses, it should be preceded by a comma unless the independent clauses are short and closely related. .......... Joseph went to Paris, **but** he stayed only three days.
Phyllis came home **and** then she left again.

| Coordinating Conjunctions | | | | | | |
|---|---|---|---|---|---|---|
| for | and | nor | but | or | yet | so |

2. A **subordinating conjunction** separates an independent clause (contains both a subject and a *verb* and can act as a complete sentence) and a dependent clause (also contains a subject and a *verb*) but does not express a complete thought. It will often show a contrast or unequal relationship. ........................................ The children *were singing*, **because** the birds *were chirping*.
Isaac *played* the guitar, **before** Dillon *played* the piano.
**Although** we *drink* water, we *enjoy drinking* lemonade.

- When a sentence consists of a dependent clause followed by an *independent clause*, the dependent clause should be followed by a comma. ............................................... **After** we left the restaurant, *we went for ice cream.*

- When a dependent clause beginning with a **subordinating conjunction** follows an *independent clause*, no comma is required. .... *The family was away* **while** the dog destroyed the flowers.

| Subordinating Conjunctions | | | |
|---|---|---|---|
| after | even though | since | whenever |
| although | how | than | wherever |
| as | if | that | whether |
| as if | in order | though | while |
| as much as | inasmuch as | unless | why |
| as though | once | until | |
| because | provided | when | |
| before | so that | where | |

3. **Correlative conjunctions** come in pairs and connect two equal grammatical items (nouns, pronouns, verbs). ............................................ We talked to **both** her parents **and** her teacher about the problems. Victor can **either** do his homework **or** miss playing games.

   - In general, correlative conjunctions do not require commas; however, they may need a comma if they join two independent clauses. ................................. **Not only** do we have to fix dinner, **but** we **also** must wash the clothes. We have not only a horse, **but** we also have a cow **and** a pig.

| Correlative Conjunctions | | | | |
|---|---|---|---|---|
| both/and | not only/but also | either/or | neither/nor | whether/or |

# Lesson 6. Conjunctions, Prepositions, and Interjections (continued)

B. A **preposition** describes a relationship between other words in a sentence. It gives information about time, place, or location.

- A **preposition** must be followed by a *noun* or *pronoun*. This is called a prepositional phrase. ........................................ The coat on the *chair* is Jorge's.
Lee is tired **from** the *hike*.
My uncle lives **in** *it*.

| Common Prepositions | | | | |
|---|---|---|---|---|
| aboard | behind | excluding | opposite | toward |
| about | below | following | outside | under |
| above | beneath | for | over | unlike |
| across | beside | from | past | underneath |
| after | between | in | per | until |
| against | beyond | inside | plus | up |
| along | but | into | regarding | upon |
| amid | by | like | round | versus |
| among | concerning | minus | save | via |
| around | considering | near | since | with |
| as | despite | of | than | within |
| at | down | off | then | without |
| before | during | on | through | |
| | except | onto | to | |

Below are some rules for prepositions:

- Do not use prepositions where they are not necessary.
  - She met ~~**up with**~~ the new coach in the hallway.
  - The book fell off ~~**of**~~ the desk.
  - He threw the book out ~~**of**~~ the window.

- When two words or phrases require the same **preposition**, the preposition does not have to be used twice.
  - You can go to the indoor pool **in** summer and ~~**in**~~ winter.

- When different **prepositions** are required, one cannot be deleted.
  - My sister was nervous **before** but happy **after** the tournament.

C. An **interjection** is a short exclamation used more in speaking than in writing. It may be followed by an exclamation mark (!) or a comma (,) when written. The most common interjections are listed in the table below.

| Interjection | Meaning | Example |
|---|---|---|
| hello | expressing greeting | **Hello,** Scott. |
| hey | calling attention | **Hey**! What is that? |
| | expressing surprise or joy | **Hey**! What a great gift! |
| hi | expressing greeting | **Hi**! How are you? |
| hmm | expressing hesitation, doubt, or disagreement | **Hmm**, I don't think that is true. |
| oh | expressing surprise, pain, or pleading | **Oh**! There you are!<br>**Oh**! I have a bruised toe!<br>**Oh!** Please can we go? |
| ouch | expressing pain | **Ouch**! That hurts! |
| well | expressing surprise or introducing a remark | **Well**! I did not do that!<br>**Well**, what do you think? |
| uh | expressing hesitation | **Uh**, is this correct? |
| uh-huh | expressing agreement | **Uh-huh**, you are right. |
| um | expressing hesitation | 9 x 6 is ... **um** ... 54. |

Read the passage and correct the conjunction, preposition, and interjection errors. There are no errors in the picture or caption.

## 25. A Profitable Platform

①②③④⑤⑥⑦⑧⑨
Conjunction
①②③④
Preposition

Dear Editor:

As part as my campaign platform for student body president, I would like to propose while students be paid for attending school. My mom is always telling me that school is my job. Students would learn much faster than usual if they got paid for it, nor they would obtain valuable experience in earning a living. Why I had been paid $5.00 for each hour I attended school last semester, I would have earned a whole lot more that I did. When my parents paid me of the two A's that I earned on my report card I only received $10. Provided should my grades improve? The school could establish neither a salary scale based on letter grades nor pay each of us students an hourly wage based to our previous semester's academic performance. I know mine would surely improve. Between the school administration gives my request due consideration, I hope that the students will be able to vote on this important issue nor things can change.

Sincerely,

Justin Case

Justin is already imagining how much money he will have for his college fund if the school votes in favor of salaries for students. "I'll earn a lot more on an hourly basis than the $5.00 for each of the two A's that I got last semester."

Optional: Use another piece of paper to rewrite the passage without errors.

Read the passage and correct the conjunction, preposition, and interjection errors. There are no errors in the picture or caption.

## 26. Making Maple Syrup

①②③④⑤⑥⑦
Conjunction
①②③④
Preposition

In the sugar bush (grove of sugar maples), farmers tap the maple trees every spring in order to catch the running sap. The sap is boiled in a sugar shanty, or shack; it takes many gallons of sap to make one gallon of maple syrup!

Large sugar bush operators now have pipeline systems, for small farmers still gather sap like sugar maple trees by hand as if that is easy! They empty the sap into a big tub nor drive it by tractor and by wagon to the sugar shanty where the liquid is boiled. It takes across forty gallons of sap to make one gallon of syrup.

Since this has been a tough year, Claire and Dave Bevy are looking for help. "You can watch and learn for us experts," they say, "so you will do well. Since you can watch and learn, so there are times you can help out. Then if you ask permission to taste the sweet and sticky samples our answer will be that you may. Once a day of making maple syrup, you will be very tired in order you will have had a lot of fun!"

Optional: Use another piece of paper to rewrite the passage without errors.

Read the passage and correct the conjunction, preposition, and interjection errors. There are no errors in the picture or caption.

## 27. Rash Results

①②③④⑤⑥⑦⑧⑨
Conjunction
①②③④
Preposition

Madeleine Vu hikes in the California hills, where, after getting a bad case of poison oak, she has learned to avoid the distinctive triple leaflets.

In the Western woods, don't be rash why you hike. You must watch out for poison oak, whether Madeleine Vu found this from the hard way while walking in California. "Poison oak is closely related to poison ivy, and it also has leaves made up for three leaflets. The plant contains oil that causes a skin reaction from you touch it. I could get poison oak not through direct contact with the plant, also through contact with anything the plant has touched. I could get it for my dog or even my clothing. As would you like to be covered over itchy red spots like mine?" Madeleine asks. "You may be sorry, or watch what's around you. Your rash will remind you for a very long time but you still need to be careful."

Optional: Use another piece of paper to rewrite the passage without errors.

Read the passage and correct the conjunction, preposition, and interjection errors. There are no errors in the picture or caption.

## 28. Rescue

①②③④⑤⑥⑦⑧
Conjunction
①②③④
Preposition

One spring day, Jorge and his friend Antonio went hiking on Mt. Mateo but it was raining. Jorge decided to take a route that looked shorter than the normal trail as though it didn't look very safe. The slope he was climbing suddenly gave way so even Jorge was caught across a rock slide. He slid 60 feet, fell for a cliff that was 15 feet high, and came to rest inside an inaccessible plateau. He had broken his leg and bruised his ribs, before he had fallen. Jorge was unable to climb the rocky slope, for he waited while Antonio went for help. Jorge was relieved although he looked of the west and saw the helicopter dropping him a lifeline. "Whether it was quite an ordeal," Jorge said of the men's experience, "he and I have learned to stick closer to the trail, because we go again."

After sliding down a rocky slope and falling 15 feet, Jorge landed a total of 75 feet from his starting point. Jorge waited for rescuers to fly in from the town in the tree-filled valley to the west.

Optional: Use another piece of paper to rewrite the passage without errors.

 

# Mini Review

# Lessons 4–6

Read the passage and correct the errors. There are no errors in the picture or caption.

## 29. A Pirate's Life for Me?

| | |
|---|---|
| ① ② | Preposition |
| ① ② ③ ④ ⑤ | Spelling |
| ① | Adverb |
| ① ② ③ ④ | Conjunction |
| ① ② ③ | Adjective |

"Yo ho, yo ho, its a pirate's life for me!" Why knot? A pirate's life was filled with adventure, danger, and much excitement! Well, that wasn't real the case. Pirates' lives were not as glamorous as books have portrayed them. Pirates made they're living attacking merchant ships and coastal towns. The batles were brutal and a pirate rarely lived longer. Pirates were considered outlaws like all nations. They sailed under their own flag, the skull and crossbones and they lived by their own loose system of rules. These rules specified the share of the treasure each pirate received, and the amount of compinsation for lost limbs and other injuries. However, very few of the pirates actually shared in the lavish treasure chests of jewels and of gold. More were very poor and many fared worst than beggars.

Pirates sailed under the skull and crossbones (a flag known as the Jolly Roger) and attacked merchant ships and towns along the North and South American coasts. In the Caribbean Sea alone, treasures worth millions of dollars lie buried beneath the waves.

Optional: Use another piece of paper to rewrite the passage without errors.

Read the passage and correct the errors. There are no errors in the picture or caption.

## 30. Do Elephants Mourn?

| | |
|---|---|
| ①②③④⑤⑥ | Spelling |
| ①② | Adjective |
| ① | Article |
| ①②③④ | Conjunction |

Do elephants mourn the loss of other elephants? Alot of scientists have wondered about this. It's a question that has no definitely answer but fascinating behaviors have been observed. There are documented cases of elephants gathering around the body of a deceased, elephant and staying with it for as long as a weak to protect it from scavengers. Seeing the remains of an tusk has prompted some elephants to stop, pick the tusk up with their trunks, caress it and then pass it among themselfs. Some elephants' have been observed trying to pick up a fallen and wounded elephant with their trunks in an attempt to help the fallen elephant to its feet again. Perhaps we will never no if elephants mourn but it is a well question to ponder. What do ewe think?

Certain behaviors suggest that elephants may have emotions similar to our own. Scientists have observed some elephants using their trunks to help lift fallen and wounded elephants.

Optional: Use another piece of paper to rewrite the passage without errors.

# Review
# Lessons 1–6

Read the passage and correct the errors. There are no errors in the picture or caption.

## 31. The Planetarium

| | |
|---|---|
| ① ② | Preposition |
| ① ② | Content |
| ① ② ③ | Capitalization |
| ① ② | Punctuation |
| ① ② | Spelling |
| ① | Article |
| ① | Adverb |
| ① | Conjunction |

Next week our class is going over a trip to the planetarium. We'll be leaving at 830 on Fri morning. I've only been there once before, so needless to say, I'm real looking forward to going back there. You can expect light-years of travel during you're visit to a planetarium. Special lights that are shon on the flat ceiling of the planetarium simulate the movements of the Stars. Music and narration help set the mood. You can enjoy a view behind the present night sky or you can see how an stars will appear in the future. On my first planetarium trip, i saw the summer sky and many other scenes. My favorite scene was this view from Earth's surface. I felt as though I was sitting on the Moon's cratered surface.

In the planetarium, lights are shone on the curved ceiling to simulate stars and planets that may be light-years away. The author's favorite scene is shown above, where the spectators feel as if they are sitting on the moon's cratered surface.

Optional: Use another piece of paper to rewrite the passage without errors.

Read the passage and correct the errors. There are no errors in the picture or caption.

## 32. Plane Scary

| | |
|---|---|
| ① ② | Content |
| ① ② | Capitalization |
| ① ② ③ ④ | Punctuation |
| ① ② | Spelling |
| ① | Adjective |
| ① | Adverb |
| ① | Conjunction |

Jan Fay parachutes to safety as her flaming biplane hurtles to the ground during the Barnstormers Air Show on Sunday, May 5.

The Barnstormers Air Show at Blue Skies Airport was heavy clouded with smoke on Saturday after Jan Fay's trimotor burst into flames. As Fay fell toward the ground a fully opened parachute appeared over her head.

"The federal Aviation Administration and the airport manager are reviewing the case," said investigator Lin. "The fact that we cant prevent air chow disasters is more unfortunate.

Jan Fay has flown for years, or piloting know longer interests her as much as constructing model airplanes. Next June she will begin her new hobby in earnest.

(Optional: Use another piece of paper to rewrite the passage without errors.)

 

Read the passage and correct the errors. There are no errors in the picture or caption.

## 33. Fishy Story

| | |
|---|---|
| ① ② | Content |
| ① ② | Capitalization |
| ① ② ③ | Punctuation |
| ① ② ③ | Spelling |
| ① ② | Adverb |
| ① | Conjunction |
| ① | Adjective |

Gerald Carter of London was picked up by Captain Chris Drake, who was sailing alone off the eastern coast of Australia. Carter was shaken, but he was relieved to be free of Wanda's jaws.

I had been diving in the south Pacific and studying the local sea life. I'm afraid I came a bit closer to a certain form of sea life than I truly desired. Lets call her Wanda. Though I moved the fast I have ever moved, I could not escape her gaping jaws. Thirtyfour teeth surrounded me and they threatened to clamp down harder at any moment. My snorkeling gear seemed to be squeezing my head most tightly than ever. My arms were just about to give out. Fortunately captain Gormand appeared and came quick to my rescue. He was able to prop Wandas' mouth open with a long beam while I escaped. Wanda is probabley now telling her friends about the won that got away!

Optional: Use another piece of paper to rewrite the passage without errors.

Read the passage and correct the errors. There are no errors in the picture or caption.

## 34. A Lesson on Haiku

| | |
|---|---|
| ① ② | Content |
| ① ② | Capitalization |
| ① ② ③ | Punctuation |
| ① ② ③ | Spelling |
| ① | Article |
| ① | Adverb |
| ① | Conjunction |

"Is this a haiku poem? Mr. Zaluski asked the class. The student's eyes scanned the poem in there literature books. "how is a haiku poem arranged?" the teacher questioned.

"An haiku poem has seventeen syllables. It's arranged in three lines of five, six, and five syllables each" Roberto replied.

"Excellent Roberto. You have been doing your homework. The haiku is a traditional form of japanese poetry that was developed in the 1700s by a man named Basho. What do you notice about haiku?" Mr. Zaluski asked.

"It's simple," Shakira stated.

"Yes, the haiku seems simple because there are few words," Mr. Zaluski replied. "However, it is meant to express something much more."

Carmen rose to the chalenge. "Maybe the poet is trying to express serenity or on the other hand, maybe the flower is meant to symbolize renewal of life."

Mr. Zaluski smiled. His class was real catching on.

Rising from the pond...
A flower spreads its petals
Taking in the sun.

--Anonymous

The poetry known as haiku was developed in the 17th century. Haiku is unrhymed and is typically based on nature or the seasons.

Optional: Use another piece of paper to rewrite the passage without errors.

# Lesson 7. Pronouns

A **pronoun** is used in place of one or more nouns. A noun is a person, place, thing, or idea. The pronoun must always agree in number and gender with the noun it replaces.

1. Do not use both a noun and a pronoun together in a sentence. .................................... Incorrect: Rover he ran away.
   Correct: Rover ran away.
   Correct: He ran away.

| Pronouns | | | | | | |
|---|---|---|---|---|---|---|
| he | him | it | my | their | us | yours |
| her | himself | itself | myself | them | we | yourself |
| hers | his | me | our | themselves | you | |
| herself | I | mine | she | they | your | |

2. A **personal pronoun** replaces one or more nouns. ..................................................... Kevin and Megan will go to the movie.
   **They** will go to the movie.

   Damian will play soccer in the stadium.
   **He** will play soccer in the stadium.

| Subjective Personal Pronouns | | | | | | |
|---|---|---|---|---|---|---|
| I | you | he | she | it | we | they |

| Objective Personal Pronouns | | | | | | |
|---|---|---|---|---|---|---|
| me | you | him | her | it | us | them |

3. Pronouns may be used as **subjects** or objects in a sentence*. ................................. **You** are being very silly.
   I will give the test results to you.

*Subjects do something. Objects receive something, and objects are usually preceded by prepositions (to, for, by, with, etc.).

- When a **pronoun** is used as the subject in a sentence, the verb must agree with the pronoun in number. .......................... They chase the ball across the yard.
  She chases the ball across the yard.

- Confusion in pronoun usage frequently occurs with compound subjects or objects. The easiest way to determine the correct form of the pronoun is to look at each member of the **compound subject** or object separately. .................................... Susan and I went to town.
  (**Susan** went to town. I went to town.)

  Tao Lai sang to her and me.
  (Tao Lai sang to her. Tao Lai sang to me.)

- **First person pronouns** (I, me/we, us) always appear last in compound subjects and objects. ..................................Rich and I watched the basketball game.

4. **I** and **me** are first person pronouns that are used in place of your name.
   - Use **I** when you are doing the action. ........I cleaned off the table.

   - Use **me** when you are receiving the action. ................................................ Felix talked to **me.**

   - To help decide when to use **I** or **me**:
     1. add an *invisible verb* to the sentence.
        Saying the verb to yourself will help you decide which word to use.

        Helen reads books better than ___ (*do*).
        Incorrect: Helen reads books better than me (*do*).
        Correct: Helen reads books better than I (*do*).

     2. leave out the noun or pronoun.
        *When in doubt, leave one out!*
        Leave out *Victoria* and then say the sentence to yourself.

        The turtle snapped at *Victoria* and _____. (I or me?)
        Incorrect: The turtle snapped at I.
        Correct: The turtle snapped at me.

# Lesson 7. Pronouns (continued)

5. A **possessive pronoun** shows ownership and never needs an apostrophe. ........................ **Hers** is the one on the left.
   The cockatoo and the parrot are **mine.**

| Possessive Pronouns | | | | | | |
|---|---|---|---|---|---|---|
| mine | yours | his | hers | its | ours | theirs |

- A **possessive pronoun** may be used before a noun to show possession or may stand alone. .................................................. **My** bike is purple and blue.
  Is the bike **mine**?

| Singular/ Plural | Person | Subjective Case | Objective Case | Possessive Case Before Noun | Possessive Case Stand Alone |
|---|---|---|---|---|---|
| singular | first person | I | me | my | mine |
| singular | second person | you | you | your | yours |
| singular | third person | he | him | his | his |
| singular | third person | she | her | her | hers |
| singular | third person | it | it | its | its |
| plural | first person | we | us | our | ours |
| plural | second person | you | you | your | yours |
| plural | third person | they | them | their | theirs |

6. A **relative pronoun** is used to start a description of a noun. This description is called an *adjective clause* (or relative clause) and comes after the noun. .................................. The baker ***who*** *made the cake* is outside.

| Relative Pronouns | | | | |
|---|---|---|---|---|
| who | whom | which | that | whose |

- **Whose** is a possessive pronoun. .................... **Whose** cell phone keeps ringing?
- Use **who** if it functions as a subject...............Is that Grady **who** is running in the hall?
- Use **whom** if it functions as the object.......... He liked his neighbor **whom** he just met.

The easiest way to decide whether to use **who** *or* **whom** (or **whoever** or **whomever**) is to mentally drop who/whom and the words preceding it and make a sentence with the words that are left by *adding he or him. If you would use he, then the sentence needs a subject, and you should use* ***who****. If you would use him, then the sentence needs an object, and you should use* ***whom****.*

Sentence: You know who/whom will be coming to dinner tonight.
Remove who/whom: *You know _______ will be coming to dinner tonight.*
Add he or him: **He** will be coming to dinner tonight.
Correct: You know **who** will be coming to dinner tonight.

OR identify the verb/action:

Sentence: You know who/whom will be coming to dinner tonight.
Try it out: **who** will be coming *or* **whom** will be coming
Correct: You know **who** will be coming to dinner tonight.

Sentence: Who/whom is the dinner for?
Remove who/whom: *is the dinner* for
Add he or him: is the dinner for **him**?
Correct: **Whom** is the dinner for?

Identify the subject and verb: subject: dinner; verb: is. Since "who" is not the subject, "whom" is the object. *The dinner is* ***for whom****?*

## Lesson 7. Pronouns (continued)

7. A **demonstrative pronoun** is used to identify people or things or to indicate spatial relationships. It is used alone (not modifying a noun). ..................................... **This** is a great restaurant!
   Is **that** an ostrich from Africa?
   **This** is my garden; **that** is my sister's garden. (**This** one is nearby; **that** one is farther away).
   **These** trees are in bloom; **those** trees are not. (**These** trees are nearby; **those** trees are farther away.)

| Demonstrative Pronouns | | | |
|---|---|---|---|
| this | that | these | those |

8. An **indefinite pronoun** does not refer to a specific person or thing.

| Indefinite Pronouns | | |
|---|---|---|
| all | everybody | no one |
| another | everyone | one |
| any | everything | other |
| anybody | few | several |
| anyone | many | some |
| anything | much | somebody |
| both | most | someone |
| each | neither | something |
| each one | nobody | such |
| either | none | |

- **Indefinite pronouns** are often used to make general statements or to indicate quantity. .. **Anybody** could make a wrong turn.
  **Many** of the children wore their coats.

- **Indefinite pronouns** use 's to form the possessive. .................................. **Nobody's** mom is driving that car!
  **Everybody's** father is talking to **everyone's** son.

- If the **indefinite pronoun** is used as a possessive with *else*, add **'s** to *else*.............. Did **anybody** *else's* ice cream melt?

9. **Reflexive** and **intensive pronouns** use the same form; they are pronouns that end in -self or -selves. They must have an antecedent (noun or pronoun) that is within the same sentence. The antecedent is the noun or noun phrase to which the pronoun refers. For example: *Charlie* thinks of himself as quite the ladies' man. The *dryer* turned itself off automatically. *I* told myself not to stay up too late.

| Reflexive and Intensive Pronouns | |
|---|---|
| myself | ourselves |
| yourself | yourselves |
| herself | themselves |
| himself | |
| itself | |

- **Reflexive pronoun**: reflects back on an antecedent (the noun or pronoun to which it refers) that is within the same sentence. ... I read by **myself.**
  We did this **ourselves.**

- **Intensive pronoun**: used to emphasize or intensify an antecedent that is next to it within the same sentence. .................... I **myself** am not going to the movie.
  He **himself** made the plane.

There is sometimes a tendency to use reflexive and intensive pronouns incorrectly in place of personal pronouns.

Incorrect: He and ***myself*** went to the mall after band practice.
(no antecedent for ***myself*** in this sentence)
Correct: He and ***I*** went to the mall after band practice.

Incorrect: They went with ***herself.*** (no antecedent for ***herself*** in this sentence)
Correct: They went with ***her.***

Read the passage and correct the pronoun errors. There are no errors in the picture or caption.

## 35. A Glimpse Into the Past

①②③④⑤⑥⑦⑧⑨ ⑩⑪ Pronoun

Tucson, Arizona

January 29, 2011

The Incas built Machu Picchu, in what is now Peru, as a mountain hideaway. It remained undiscovered until 1911.

Dear Linda,

I haven't written since mine letter of December 22, 2010, because I've been busy writing a report about Machu Picchu. This hidden city is 8,000 feet high and was built by the Incas in South America. The Incas were conquered in the 1500s, but another of they fled to this secret city. He remained undiscovered for about another 400 years. I read and am sending you "Secrets of the Past," an article that gives we many facts about the ruins. It shows a stone wall with a man whom is only a third as tall. I also read, "Inca Treasures," a popular story about an Inca man. No one liked the story but them learned more from the article. All gave me a glimpse to the world of the Incas. They lives were far different from our in Tucson, Arizona, today!

Your friend,

Azzi

Optional: Use another piece of paper to rewrite the passage without errors.

Read the passage and correct the pronoun errors. There are no errors in the picture or caption.

## 36. An Early American

①②③④⑤⑥⑦⑧⑨⑩⑪⑫ Pronoun

Us could hardly wait to hear the author of "Early American Animals!" "Had you lived during the 1830s, your might have seen great herds of bison grazing between the Appalachian Mountains and the Rockies," he began. "Though everyone of these majestic creatures were wiped out, they are still around today."

We interrupted his. "How would you know a pair of bison if they themself walked down your street?" we asked.

"Well," he answered, "few bison's hair is coarse and brown. Those have a hump on their back. Two horns adorn each massive head, and the bison wear beards under theirs chins. A bull weighs close to a ton, but a cow weighs half as much. When provoked, no one of the two bison could probably run quite fast. Let's hope me would run the fastest!"

We were glad that ours hero had both knowledge and a sense of humor.

According to "Early American Animals," what we call the American buffalo is more correctly identified as the bison. The males are bulls, and the females are cows. Males often weigh nearly 2,000 pounds, and females weigh about 1,000 pounds. Bison have dark brown coats and rough hair.

Optional: Use another piece of paper to rewrite the passage without errors.

Read the passage and correct the pronoun errors. There are no errors in the picture or caption.

## 37. Animated About Art

①②③④⑤⑥⑦⑧⑨⑩⑪⑫ Pronoun

Our were excited to hear about jobs at Magic Carpet Studios! We readily lent us ears to Supervisor Warren of the animation team. "Layout artists make sketches of his scenes for the animated film. Background artists create tone and style, and each animator designs a character. Have me any idea how much research is necessary for the animator's job?" he asked.

We told he that we already knew of artists who practically lived with deer to learn them movements.

"The animators draw the extreme movements," his continued, "but the inbetweeners make all the intermediate drawings. Finally, our is the cleanup artist whom draws the most carefully of all. These who redraw, must add the final touches. For example," he said, as he pointed at a pig's suspenders, "these two buttons must be added at cleanup. It is the cleanup artist that work will be seen by me, the audience."

The animation supervisor described various artists' tasks, as listed below. The scene above was used to illustrate the cleanup artist's job.

- layout artist: sketch of scenes
- background artist: overall tone and style
- animator: characters, extreme movements
- inbetweener: intermediate movements
- cleanup artist: painstaking detail work

Optional: Use another piece of paper to rewrite the passage without errors.

Read the passage and correct the pronoun errors. There are no errors in the picture or caption.

## 38. Footnotes In Anatomy

① ② ③ ④ ⑤ ⑥ ⑦ ⑧ ⑨ ⑩ ⑪ Pronoun

"Next, we're going to discuss the human foot, which has 26 bones in both," said Mrs. Langdon. "Them can be divided into three different kinds." As she pointed at the ankle, Mrs. Langdon asked, "Can other give the name for the ankle bones?" Becky answered that they were the tarsals. "That's right," Mrs. Langdon said. "The foot has seven tarsal bones. What about the instep bones?" Miguel correctly identified they as the metatarsals. "These's right again," Mrs. Langdon said. "The foot has five metatarsal bones. Whom knows what we call the bones in ours toes?" Anybody knew, except Mrs. Langdon himself, so she continued. "The toe bones are called phalanges. The foot has fourteen phalanges. Two are in the big toe, and three are in either of the other four toes. Can any guess why the big toe has one fewer bone than the rest of the toes? Oh, there's the bell. We'll have to take up that subject on Monday. Have a great weekend!"

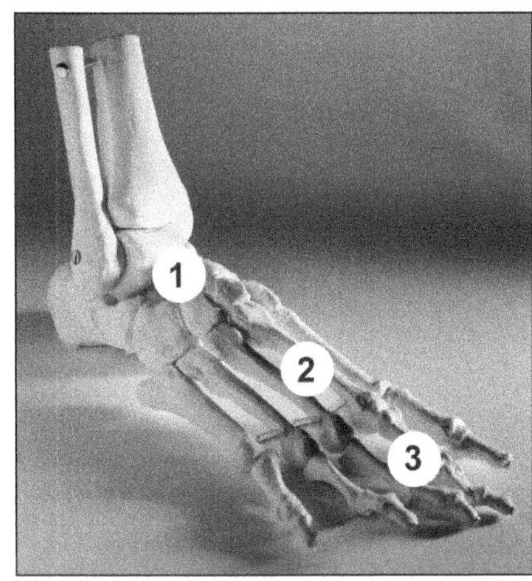


The human foot has 26 bones, which can be divided into three categories: (1) tarsals, (2) metatarsals, and (3) phalanges, pronounced fuh-lan-jees.

Optional: Use another piece of paper to rewrite the passage without errors.

# Lesson 8. Verbs

A **verb** is used to describe an action, state, or occurrence. Every sentence must have a verb

A. All verbs have four principal parts:

1. **present tense (base verb)**
   (the main verb itself) ........................................ I saw you **skip** rope.
   Please **answer** the phone.

   - When *to* is added before the verb, it is called an **infinitive**. It is used as a noun, adjective, or adverb. ..................................... **To sleep** is all Eli wants after finals. (noun)
     Melissa always brings a book **to read.** (adjective)
     Joe braved the snow **to save** the kitten. (adverb)

2. **present participle** (add *-ing* to the base verb and use a helping verb before to form verb phrases). .................................................. Sean is **watch*ing*** the football game.
   I am **driv*ing*** very slowly.

3. **past tense**
   - **Regular** verbs form the past tense or past participle by adding *-d* or *-ed* to the verb. ..... They **mov*ed*** into a new home.
     The girl **walk*ed*** three miles.

   - **Irregular** verbs are spelled differently or stay the same to form the past tense or past participle. .......................................... The pipe just **burst.**
     The pipe **burst** yesterday.

     Did Tess **bring** her dog with her?
     Tess **brought** her dog with her.

4. **past participle** (add *-d* or *-ed* to the base verb and use a helping verb before to form verb phrases). .......................................................... Pascal had **complet*ed*** his chores.
   The puppy was **frighten*ed*.**

*a past tense verb used with a helping verb (has, have, or had

 

| Regular Verbs | | | |
|---|---|---|---|
| Present Tense | Present Participle | Past Tense | Past Participle |
| care | caring | cared | cared |
| call | calling | called | called |
| jump | jumping | jumped | jumped |
| walk | walking | walked | walked |
| bake | baking | baked | baked |
| dance | dancing | danced | danced |
| instruct | instructing | instructed | instructed |

| Irregular Verbs | | | |
|---|---|---|---|
| Present Tense | Present Participle | Past Tense | Past Participle |
| bring | bringing | brought | brought |
| choose | choosing | chose | chosen |
| go | going | went | gone |
| ride | riding | rode | ridden |
| think | thinking | thought | thought |
| fall | falling | fell | fallen |
| know | knowing | knew | known |
| cut | cutting | cut | cut |
| do | doing | did | done |
| build | building | built | built |
| burst | bursting | burst | burst |
| lend | lending | lent | lent |
| pay | paying | paid | paid |
| shrink | shrinking | shrank (or shrunk) | shrunk (or shrunken) |

## Lesson 8. Verbs (continued)

B. A verb phrase consists of a base **verb** and one or more *helping verbs* (also called auxiliary verbs). .................................................. Grandma and Grandpa *are* **coming** to visit.
I *will have* **gone** to school by then.

- Helping verbs are part of a verb phrase. Many verb tenses are formed by using helping verbs.

| Common Helping Verbs | | | | | | | | | | | |
|---|---|---|---|---|---|---|---|---|---|---|---|
| be | can | could | do | have | may | might | must | shall | should | will | would |

| Tense | Verb Phrase | Example |
|---|---|---|
| Present Perfect | have or has + past participle | Amanda has baked a cake. |
| Past Perfect | had + past participle | Amanda had baked a cake. |
| Future Perfect | will (or shall) have + past participle | Amanda will have baked a cake. |
| Present Progressive | be (present) + present participle | Amanda is baking a cake. |
| Past Progressive | be (past) + present participle | Amanda was baking a cake. |
| Future Progressive | will or shall + be (base form) + present participle | Amanda will be baking a cake. |
| Future Tense | will or shall + base form | Amanda will bake a cake. |

C. **Verb tense** tells whether an action is happening now, has already happened, or will happen in the future. .................................... I **ride** the bus home. (happening now)
I **rode** the bus home yesterday. (has already happened)
I *will* **ride** the bus home tomorrow.(will happen in the future)

- The only difference between the **simple tenses** and the **perfect tenses** is that in the perfect tense the action has been completed or finished. ..................................

I **call** my sister often. (simple present)
I **called** my sister often. (simple past)
I *will* **call** my sister often. (simple future)
I *have* **called** my sister often. (present perfect)
I *had* **called** my sister often. (past perfect)
I *will have* **called** my sister often. (future perfect)

- A verb can also have special forms to show that the action is continuing. These forms are called the **progressive forms**. They are made by using some form of the verb *to be* with the **present participle** (a word formed by adding -ing and using a helping verb). .........

I *am* **building** a house.
I *was* **building** a house.
I *will be* **building** a house.

- The **present participle** is used with a form of the verb *be* in the progressive tense. The form of *be* determines whether the sentence is present or past progressive. .....................

The boy *is* **flying** a kite. (present progressive)
The boy *was* **flying** a kite. (past progressive)
The kite *was* **flown**. (adjective)

- The **past participle** is used with a form of the verb *be* in passive voice. The form of *be* determines whether the sentence is present or past progressive. ...........................

A kite *is* **flown** by the boy. (present progressive)
A kite *was* **flown** by the boy. (past progressive)

- The **past participles** of both **do** and **go** are always used with a *helping verb* to create the present perfect, the past perfect, and the future perfect tenses. ........................................

Mom *has* **done** the puzzle. (present perfect)
Mom *had* **done** the puzzle. (past perfect)
Mom *will have* **done** the puzzle. (future perfect)

Meg *has* **gone** to the store. (present perfect)
Meg *had* **gone** to the store. (past perfect)
Meg *will have* **gone** to the store. (future perfect)

## Lesson 8. Verbs (continued)

- The present and past tenses can be further subdivided into the emphatic tense which is used to give greater emphasis. The **present emphatic tense** is formed by using *do* or *does* with the base verb. ............................................ I *do* **like** my new dress.
  He *does* **run** fast.
  - The **past emphatic tense** is formed by using the past tense of *do* with the base verb. .......... I *did* **eat** all the cherries.
    He *did* **run** fast.

| Tense | Verb Phrase | Example |
|---|---|---|
| present tense | Active: base verb<br>(Passive: be + past participle) | Active: I ask him.<br>(Passive: He is asked.) |
| present progressive | be + present participle | I am asking |
| present emphatic | do + base verb | I do ask. |
| present perfect tense | have or has + past participle | I have asked. |
| present perfect progressive | have or has + be (past participle) + present participle | I have been asking |
| past tense | Active: past<br>(Passive: be [past] and past participle) | Active: I asked him.<br>(Passive: He was asked.) |
| past progressive | be (past) + present participle | I was asking |
| past emphatic | do (past) + base verb | I did ask. |
| past perfect tense | had + past participle | I had asked. |
| past perfect progressive | had + be (past participle) + present participle | I had been asking. |
| future tense | Active: will or shall + base verb<br>(Passive: will or shall + be + past participle | Active: I will ask him.<br>(Passive: He will be asked.) |
| future progressive | will or shall + be (bare infinitive) + present participle | I will be asking. |
| future perfect tense | will (or shall) have + past participle | I will have asked. |
| future perfect progressive | will (or shall) have + be (past participle) + present participle | I will have been asking. |

D. **Verb Voice**

- **Active voice**: The subject performs an action. ... Lamont **chased** the cats.
Alex **slammed** the door.
Renee **ate** Elizabeth's chips.

- **Passive voice**: The subject receives an action. *State of being (linking) verbs* link a noun, pronoun, or adjective to the subject. .................. The cats *were* **chased** by Lamont.
The door *was* **slammed** by Alex.
Elizabeth's chips *were* **eaten** by Renee.

| Common State of Being Verbs | | | | | | | | | |
|---|---|---|---|---|---|---|---|---|---|
| am | appear | be | been | become | feel | grow | is | look | remain |
| seem | smell | sound | stay | taste | was | were | | | |

- Some state of being (linking) verbs can also be used as action verbs. To help decide whether the verb is being used as a state of being verb or an action verb, substitute the appropriate form of *is* and *seem* for the **verb**. If the sentence still makes sense and has not changed its meaning, then the verb is a state of being verb. ...........................He **remains** happy. (He *is* happy. He *seems* happy.) The meaning has not changed.

Remains is a state of being (linking) verb, linking to the adjective happy.

He **remains** happily at the park. (He *is* happily at the park. He *seems* happily at the park.) The meaning has changed.

Remains is an action verb. The adverb happily describes remains.

# Lesson 8. Verbs (continued)

Below are examples of active and passive voice in various tenses:

| Tense | Active Voice | Passive Voice |
|---|---|---|
| present | The dog chases the birds. | The birds are chased by the dog. |
| present perfect | The dog has chased the birds. | The birds have been chased by the dog. |
| past | The dog chased the birds. | The birds were chased by the dog. |
| past perfect | The dog had chased the birds. | The birds had been chased by the dog. |
| future | The dog will chase the birds. | The birds will be chased by the dog. |
| future perfect | The dog will have chased the birds. | The birds will have been chased by the dog. |
| present progressive | The dog is chasing the birds. | The birds are being chased by the dog. |
| present perfect progressive | The dog has been chasing the birds. | |
| past progressive | The dog was chasing the birds. | The birds were being chased by the dog. |
| past perfect progressive | The dog had been chasing the birds. | |
| future progressive | The dog will be chasing the birds. | |
| future perfect progressive | The dog will have been chasing the birds. | |

## E. Verb Moods

- **Indicative mood** expresses a fact or opinion. ..... Charles **is** funny.
  Ashley **feels** hungry.
  Louie **looks** out of the window.

- **Imperative mood** expresses a command or request (implied subject is "you"). ........................ (You) **Show** me where you put it.
  **Set** the table.
  **Bring** me my socks.
  **Hold** the door open.

- **Interrogative mood** asks a question or requests information or an action (expressed subject). .... Will you **show** me where you put it?
  Will they **set** the table?
  Will she **bring** me my socks?
  Will he **hold** the door open?

- **Conditional mood** suggests what *might, could,* or *would* happen if something occurs. ............... Laura *might* **feel** tired later if she doesn't **take** a nap.
  Kyrone *could* **go** to the movies if he **likes** what is showing.
  Eric *would* **help** if he **was** not **busy.**

- **Subjunctive mood** suggests something contrary to fact, wishful, hypothetical, or imaginary. .................................................. If Monique **were** here, then we would be laughing.
  If Frank **were** a teacher, then he would have summers off.
  If Lenora **had studied,** then she would have passed the class.
  If Zoe **had worn** sunscreen, then she would not have gotten burned.
  If it **had been** me, I wouldn't have been there in the first place.
  If it **had been** before 10:30, I could have ordered breakfast.

Read the passage and correct the verb errors. There are no errors in the picture or caption.

## 39. Predators Beware

①②③④⑤⑥⑦⑧
⑨⑩ Verb

The llama is related to the camel. Llamas have no hooves but will use their large feet to attack the enemy. The llama above has just kicked a coyote that threatened the sheep herd.

The llama is a relative of the camel. Although the llama had many similarities to the camel, the most noticeable difference between the two be that the llama doesn't have a hump on its back. In South American countries, llamas are often use as pack animals. In the U.S., people are found other uses for llamas. Some sheep ranchers will use llamas to guard their flocks. Llamas grazing in the fields with the sheep and will think of them as their herd. If the sheep are attack, a llama will be rushing at the attacker and strike with its large feet. It will also spit saliva into the attacker's face.

"Llamas are effective as the sheep's protectors," says rancher Giselle Robinson, "because they were reducing the number of sheep lost to predators. Overall, I'd say that we get along with llamas extremely well."

Optional: Use another piece of paper to rewrite the passage without errors.

Read the passage and correct the verb errors. There are no errors in the picture or caption.

## 40. Camera Shy

① ② ③ ④ ⑤ ⑥ ⑦ ⑧
⑨ ⑩ ⑪ ⑫ Verb

A hammerhead shark objected to its photograph being took and sent two scuba divers swim for cover. The divers, scientists with the National Oceanographic Society, are taking pictures for an upcoming article featuring the hammerhead's uniquely shaped head. After slowly circling the divers, the shark suddenly tried butt them with its head. Bob Noble, the diver was arm with a shark dart, has made it into the diving cage first. Brian Black, the second diver, will drop both his camera and his flipper as he swim to safety. If the shark had swims faster than Noble and Black, they might not have been so lucky. Hammerhead sharks have known to attack people, and the scientists leaving nothing to chance. "Next time, we get his permission first," said the shaken Mr. Black.

Two divers are attacked while photographing a hammerhead shark. The diver armed with the shark dart makes it into the diving cage first. Although the second man loses two pieces of equipment, he saves his skin.

Optional: Use another piece of paper to rewrite the passage without errors.

Read the passage and correct the verb errors. There are no errors in the picture or caption.

## 41. The Giant of His Age

①②③④⑤⑥⑦⑧⑨⑩ Verb

Leonardo da Vinci was a painter, a sculptor, a mathematician, a scientist, an engineer, a philosopher, and many other things. He was knowed in popular culture for his paintings, including many that are still widely recognize. His most famous painting was the Mona Lisa. In his day, he is known for providing early models of technological advances that include the airplane, the automobile, and the parachute. He also proposing using simple machines, such as pulleys and levers, to have done complex tasks. One of his ideas was the wheel-driven machine, which uses the turning of a wheel to produce energy. During the Industrial Revolution, factories begun using this wheel-driven technology to produce hydroelectric power. In addition, da Vinci was famous for his enormous number of drawings of the human body, including illustrations of the functions of bones and organs. His drawings been considered to be the first accurate portrayals of human anatomy. Because of the many contributions to our progress, da Vinci was a man to whom we did owe many thanks.

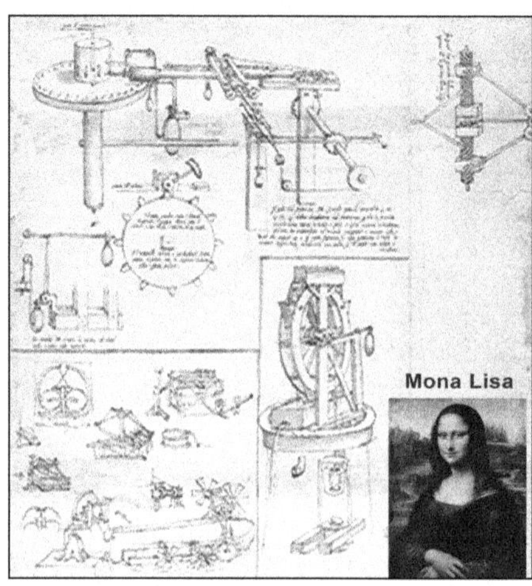


Above are shown Leonardo da Vinci's most famous painting and some drawings for a wheel-driven machine. During the Industrial Revolution, factories began using this wheel-driven technology to produce hydroelectric power.

Optional: Use another piece of paper to rewrite the passage without errors.

Read the passage and correct the verb errors. There are no errors in the picture or caption.

## 42. The Gentle Sea Cow

① ② ③ ④ ⑤ ⑥ ⑦ ⑧ ⑨ ⑩ Verb

The manatee, or sea cow, be the only herbivorous mammal that will lives entirely in the water. The manatee can grow to be 14 feet long and can weigh up to 1,500 pounds. Manatees do graze on underwater plants and can stay underwater for up to 30 minutes. The upper lip of the manatee been divided into two parts. It used these two halves as pinchers to grab water plants. It can ate more than 100 pounds of plants per day! The manatee likes warm coastal waters and, in the U.S., inhabited the bays and rivers of Florida. In some parts of Florida and South America, manatees uses to keep waterways free of weeds. The gentle manatee be an endangered species. The encyclopedia article "Sea Cows," in fact, reports that one manatee, the Stellar's sea cow, was hunts to extinction twenty-seven years after it was discovered!

The gentle, herbivorous manatee lives in warm coastal waters. Manatees can grow to be 14 feet long and weigh up to 1,500 pounds. They can stay underwater for up to half an hour and eat more than 100 pounds of plants per day! In some parts of Florida and South America, manatees are used to keep waterways free of weeds.

Optional: Use another piece of paper to rewrite the passage without errors.

# Lesson 9. Clauses and Phrases

A. A **clause** is a group of words containing a subject and a verb. There are two types of clauses: independent (main) and dependent (subordinate).

1. An independent clause (main clause) has a subject and a verb. It can stand alone as a simple sentence by adding an *initial capital* and **ending punctuation**. ............................... she is older than her brother
   She is older than her brother.

   - A sentence can contain more than one independent clause. .................................... It was a hot and humid day, and I needed a cool drink.

2. A dependent clause (subordinate) cannot stand alone. It is not a complete thought. ................. where my bother had gone

   - A dependent clause has to be combined with an **independent clause** to form a sentence. ... **We knew** where my brother had gone.
     **We wondered** whom he was seeing.

3. Recognizing independent and dependent clauses is useful when punctuating sentences.

   - independent clause + independent clause
     - Use a **comma** after the first clause when the clauses are joined by a *coordinating conjunction*. ......................... The sun was shining brightly**,** *and* the weather was warm.
     - Use a **semicolon** after the first clause when the clauses are not joined by a coordinating conjunction. ......................... The sun was shining brightly**;** the weather was warm.

   - *dependent clause* + independent clause
     Use a **comma** after the dependent clause. ... *After we left for the country*, the package we were waiting for arrived.

- independent clause + *dependent clause*
  It depends whether the dependent clause is **essential** or **nonessential**.

  - An **essential** clause gives information that is needed to the sentence. Removing it would change the meaning of the sentence. A comma is not required. .......................... The cars stopped **when the officer** blew his whistle.

  - A **nonessential** clause can be removed without altering the meaning of the sentence. Nonessential clauses give additional or incidental information, but are not necessary to the basic idea of the sentence. ............................................. The cars stopped when the officer, **who was on duty**, blew his whistle.

4. A sentence will not contain two *dependent clauses* without an independent clause. ........ Incorrect: *if it rains when you arrive*
   Correct: I will pick you up at the station *if it rains when you arrive.*

B. A **phrase** is a group of words that act as a unit and contain either a subject or a verb but not both. ................................................ **leaving behind the dog**

1. A phrase cannot stand alone. It must always be part of a sentence. ............... Walking to the park was fun.
   The dog was running quickly.
   That is the prettiest flower in the garden.

2. A phrase may be located anywhere in a sentence, but when it begins a sentence, it is usually followed by a **comma**. ..................... When safely home, they felt relieved.
   In the spring, I will plant a garden.

## Lesson 9. Clauses and Phrases (continued)

C. **Dangling** and **Misplaced Modifiers**
A **modifier** is a word or phrase that adds detail or description to a sentence. ................................ **We slowly ate the lunch** that we had brought.

1. A **dangling modifier** occurs when the subject of the modifier is unclear.

   Incorrect: **Looking toward the west**, a funnel-shaped cloud stirred up dust.
   (This suggests the cloud is doing the looking.)
   Correct: Looking toward the west, I saw a funnel-shaped cloud stirring up dust.
   (This is clear that I was looking toward the west.)

   Incorrect: **When nine years old**, my mother enrolled in medical school.
   (This suggests my mother enrolled in medical school when she was nine.)
   Correct: When I was nine years old, my mother enrolled in medical school.)
   (This is clear I was nine years old when my mother enrolled in medical school.)

2. A **misplaced modifier** occurs when the subject of the modifier is unclear because the modifier is poorly placed.

   Incorrect: Becky ate a **cold bowl** of cereal for breakfast.
   (This suggests that the bowl was cold.)
   Correct: Becky ate a bowl of **cold cereal** for breakfast.
   (This is clear that the cereal was cold.)

   Incorrect: They saw a fence behind the **house made of barbed wire.**
   (This suggests that the house was made of barbed wire.)
   Correct: They saw a fence **made of barbed wire** behind the house.
   (This is clear that the fence was made of barbed wire.)

Read the passage and correct the clause and phrase errors. There are no errors in the picture or caption.

## 43. Night Fright

① ② ③ ④ ⑤ ⑥ ⑦ ⑧
⑨ ⑩ Clause/Phrase

Deep in the night she heard the sound of water roaring through the hallway. Saraya peeked out her door. The hallway was as dry now as it had been when she arrived earlier that day. It was even deeper in the night when she heard the horrible scream. She called out and her voice echoed in the silence. It was almost dawn for the sun was trying to rise when she felt her bed shake. She jumped up she threw open the door and ran into the hall. Trying to ignore the intensifying screech behind her she zoomed down the long stairway and into the courtyard. She considered climbing over the wall that surrounded the castle that was made of ashlar, but decided against it. Frantic, she ran along the wall until she stumbled and fell. She heard the noise right behind her and then she turned around to face her fate. There stood her brother who had a big grin on his face holding a cell phone that was playing "Sounds in the Night."

"That's not fair, Mohammed!" Saraya cried. Mohammed just laughed. "We'll leave tomorrow. You'll see," Saraya said, planning to ask Mom and Dad to cut the visit short.

On the morning before Saraya's fright, her family arrived at this Scottish castle made of stone for a two-week vacation.

Optional: Use another piece of paper to rewrite the passage without errors.

Read the passage and correct the clause and phrase errors. There are no errors in the picture or caption.

## 44. The Monarch

In the spring butterflies seem to be everywhere but where do they live during the winter? In autumn, flocks of North American monarch butterflies migrate south. To milder climates One of their destinations is Pacific Grove, California where they will remain until spring. They hibernate in trees in the parks and surrounding areas. In some areas special butterfly habitats have been set aside to protect these yearly visitors. When you visit these habitats, hanging from the trees you see what look like large clusters of dried leaves. In fact these clusters are hundreds of butterflies with their wings closed. The dull under part of the monarch's wing resembles a dead leaf it provides the butterfly with protective camouflage when it is resting. The butterflies hang down in overlapping layers. From the tree branches They will hibernate this way until spring arrives. When the butterflies' wings are warmed by the sun they will begin to fly again.

Few North American butterflies can live through the cold winter. They usually migrate to warmer climates in the southern United States and Central America. Each year, monarchs and other butterflies spend the winter hibernating in trees, barns, and other dark, sheltered places until spring.

Optional: Use another piece of paper to rewrite the passage without errors.

Read the passage and correct the clause and phrase errors. There are no errors in the picture or caption.

## 45. A Sucker for Squid

① ② ③ ④ ⑤ ⑥ ⑦ ⑧
⑨ ⑩ ⑪ Clause/Phrase

A hidden video camera finally captured. The thief who'd been stealing the octopus food. Over the last few days a lab assistant had noticed something strange. Each morning, pieces of squid were missing. From the jar of food kept near the octopus tank. He set up a hidden video camera one night to monitor the lab in a light fixture. The next day the mystery was solved. The octopus had found a small opening in the cover of its tank. During the night it would squeeze through the opening. Like all octopuses it was able to compress all of its body except the mouth. Fortunately for the octopus the opening was large enough for its mouth to fit through. It slid its tentacles through first and then it pulled the rest of its body through the opening. Using the suckers on its arms, the octopus had then grasped the lid of the jar, pulled it off, removed a piece of squid, and proceeded to snack. When it was done eating the octopus climbed back. Inside the tank.

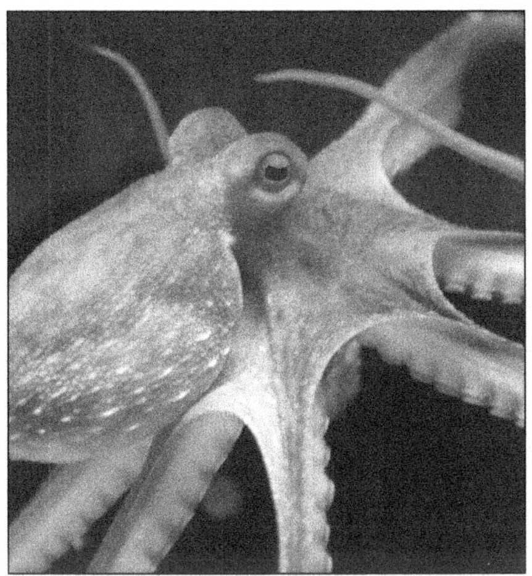

Along each of its arms, an octopus has suckers that it uses to grasp things. The only hard part on an octopus's body is its mouth, which is similar to a bird's beak. The rest of the octopus's body is made of soft tissue that can be easily compressed.

Optional: Use another piece of paper to rewrite the passage without errors.

Read the passage and correct the clause and phrase errors. There are no errors in the picture or caption.

## 46. Heart-Racing Journey

①②③④⑤⑥⑦⑧⑨
Clause/Phrase

With the goal of studying a microscopic society I prepare for transport. I am successfully shrunk but something has gone wrong with the coordinates! I materialize. In the right atrium of a chambered muscular organ. What could have happened? Suddenly, all is still and I brace for a contraction. The jolt hurls the blood cells and me past the tricuspid valve into the right ventricle. Hey, I have somehow survived! The ventricle squeezes the blood and me toward the lungs. Where I can be saved. Our engineer will surely locate and beam me out. Once I'm there. I am propelled with a rush but slow down just at the pulmonary valve. While struggling to escape, the three cusps trap me like doors! I am not to be defeated, though. With a mighty effort I pull my hips through and then my legs, too. I am free of the heart! I glide to the lungs I am sure I will soon be saved.

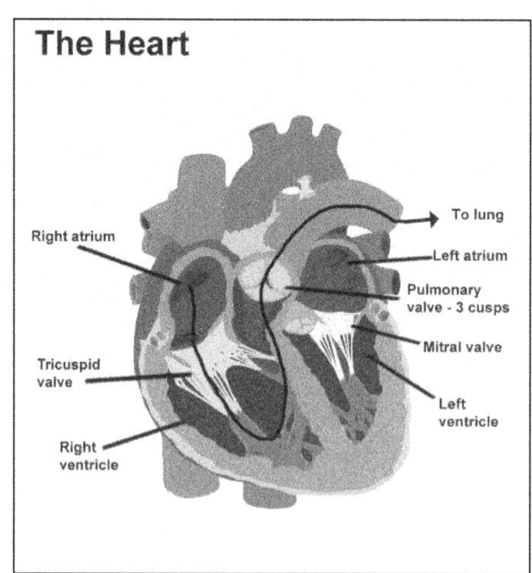


The black arrow shows the path of the hapless investigator, who was finally identified in a lung, relocated to the transport room of the mother ship, and maximized in size.

Optional: Use another piece of paper to rewrite the passage without errors.

# Mini Review
# Lessons 7–9

Read the passage and correct the errors. There are no errors in the picture or caption.

## 47. The Eagle Nebula

①②③ Pronoun
①②③④ Verb
①②③④⑤ Clause/Phrase

As me clicked through the television channels, I favorite science show appear. Launched in 1990, the announcer was saying, "The Hubble Space Telescope has recorded many astounding images for none on Earth. One such image be this picture inside the Milky Way galaxy of the Eagle Nebula." A brilliant vision of the nebula fill my screen as he continued. "Radiation from nearby stars causes these enormous towers. Of gas and dust to glow. You noticed the globules of gas at the top of the leftmost tower. Each glob may contain newly forming stars about the size of our solar system!" Wow! Where else could I learn as much as I do. From "Outer Visions"?

Here is the image that appeared on "Outer Visions." These pillars of gas and dust belong to the Eagle Nebula, residing in our Milky Way. They were revealed by the Hubble Space Telescope, placed in orbit in 1990.

Optional: Use another piece of paper to rewrite the passage without errors.

Read the passage and correct the errors. There are no errors in the picture or caption.

## 48. America's First Colony

①②③④ Pronoun
①②③④ Verb
①②③④ Clause/Phrase

Jamestown, founded in 1607 was the first permanent English colony in America. A group of English investors formed the London Company to seek profit in the new land. Them sent Capt. John Smith and a group of settlers to establish a colony in what is now Virginia. The new settlers struggle with hunger, disease, and attacks. By the natives. The greatest of these threats to the little settlement's survival was disease. Even with the arrival of two additional groups of settlers the population declined. The settlers are determined, however, to survive. Many were indentured servants for who there was no going back. They had sold them labor to the new land in exchange for free passage. Four years after the founding, the London Company gave each colonist a parcel of land. Another of the colonists started raising tobacco. This prove to be a very profitable crop, and the colony finally begin to thrive.

In 1607, Captain John Smith established Jamestown, which became the first lasting English colony in America. In 1611, the settlers were given their own land and started growing tobacco.

(Optional: Use another piece of paper to rewrite the passage without errors.)

# Lesson 10. Agreement

## A. Subject With a Verb

A **subject** and a **verb** must agree. Both must be singular or both must be plural.

1. Use a **singular verb** with a singular subject (noun or pronoun). ................................ Eli's brother **goes** to college.
   He **watches** soccer whenever he can.

2. Use a **plural verb** with a plural subject. .......... Those girls **play** in a band.
   They **eat** ice cream.

3. Use a **plural verb** with I and you. .................... I **go** to tennis practice tomorrow.
   You **will go** to Miles' house tomorrow.
   All three of you **go** to the end of the line.

4. The **verb** should agree with the subject even when the subject and the verb are inverted. ..... Performing for the first time today **is** Winifred Lowell.
   Performing for the first time today **are** the Lowell sisters.

5. The agreement between the subject and **verb** is not usually affected by any *phrases* that fall between the subject and the verb. ..................... The difficulties of *going on a long trip* **were** obvious.
   The difficulty of *going on a trip* **was** obvious.

**Note:** The only exception to this rule is a verb with an indefinite pronoun. See below.

## B. Verb With Indefinite Pronoun

The **verb** must agree with the **indefinite pronoun** in number.

1. Singular indefinite pronouns use a **singular verb**. ................................................ Everybody **has** a car.
   Somebody **is** home.
   Nobody **likes** being yelled at.

2. Plural indefinite pronouns use a **plural verb**. ..................................................... Few birds **were** in the park.
   Both students **know** the answer.
   Many **eat** lunch in the cafeteria.

## Lesson 10. Agreement (continued)

3. Depending on the *subject*, the following words may be singular or plural: some, any, none, all, and most. ........................ Some of the *paper* is torn.
   Some of the *papers* are torn.

   All of the *house* is painted brown.
   All of the *houses* are painted brown.

   Most of the *car* is dirty.
   Most of the *cars* are dirty.

C. **Pronoun With Antecedent**

1. A **pronoun** must agree with its antecedent in number, gender, and person. The antecedent is the noun or noun phrase to which the pronoun refers. ............................ The boy flew the kite.
   Incorrect: **She** flew the kite.
   Correct: **He** flew the kite.

   A llama will charge and strike with its large feet.
   Incorrect: **They** will charge and strike with its large feet.
   Correct: **It** will charge and strike with its large feet.

2. A **possessive pronoun** must agree with its antecedent. ................................ Incorrect: An artist is admired for **their** skill with a brush.
   Correct: An artist is admired for **his** or **her** skill with a brush.

D. **Adjective With Noun or Pronoun**

1. An adjective and the **noun or pronoun** it modifies must agree in number. ........................ Incorrect: Marsha has one **sisters.**
   Correct: Marsha has two **sisters.**

2. When **this**, **that**, **these**, or **those** are used as adjectives, they must agree in number with the noun or pronoun they are modifying. ............... Incorrect: **This** vegetables are cold.
   Correct: **These** vegetables are cold.
   Correct: **Those** vegetables are cold.
   Incorrect: **These** dog and **those** cat are friends.
   Correct: **This** dog and **that** cat are friends.

## E. Verb With Compound Subject

**Compound subjects** are formed by joining words or groups of words with *and*, *or*, or *nor*.

1. **Subjects** joined with *and* take a plural verb. This is true whether the words making up the compound subject are singular or plural. ......... Our **cat** *and* **dog** spend a lot of time in the yard.
   Our **cats** *and* **dogs** spend a lot of time in the yard.

2. Sometimes *and* is used to connect two subjects that function as a **unit** to name a single item. In these cases, the subject is not a compound subject. ........................................... **Macaroni** *and* **cheese** is my favorite dish.
   **Stop** *and* **Go** was the name of the market.
   **Peanut butter** *and* **jelly** gives me energy.

3. **Singular subjects** joined by *or* or *nor* use a singular verb. ........................... Either this **week** *or* next **week** is fine with me.
   A **chair** *or* a **stool** fits under the counter.
   Neither **Melissa** *nor* **Jody** plays the clarinet.

4. When plural subjects are joined with *or* or *nor*, they take a **plural verb**. ................... Jackets *or* sweaters **are** needed at night.
   Either his parents *or* my parents **take** us to school.
   Neither our cats *nor* our dogs **enjoy** having baths.

5. When a **singular subject** and a **plural subject** are joined by *or* or *nor*, the verb agrees in number with the subject closer to the verb. ..................... A sports **coat** *or* evening **clothes** are required.
   Evening **clothes** *or* a sports **coat** is required.

   Either the **boys** *or* their **uncle** drives the van.
   Either their **uncle** *or* the **boys** drive the van.

   Neither the **doctor** *nor* the **nurses** were feeling well.
   Neither the **nurses** *nor* the **doctor** is feeling well.

Read the passage and correct the agreement errors. There are no errors in the picture or caption.

## 49. Let the Chips Fall

① ② ③ ④ ⑤ ⑥ ⑦ ⑧ ⑨ ⑩ Agreement

Harold is getting ready to bake a batch of cookies for Lisa to take to the carnival. He finds a recipe for chocolate chip cookies and read it thoughtfully. Harold decide to add more chocolate chips and less flour so that the cookies will taste even better. He double the amount of chips and halves the flour. He puts one cup of flour into the bowl and adds the other dry ingredients. He carefully breaks and adds the two eggs and mixes in the remaining ingredients. He spoons the batter onto a greased cookie sheet and lay the sheet in the oven to bake for the required ten minutes. He takes the cookies out of the oven when the timer goes off. The cookies is melted chocolate blobs. “Well, I can’t sends this cookies to the carnival. Surely, nobody want these,” says Harold, “but it won’t go to waste.” Harold knows to whom she will give the chocolate mass. “By tonight, Lisa will have tasted my new recipe for chocolate candy!”

Harold uses the recipe above in his attempt to make chocolate chip cookies. He alters only the amounts of chocolate chips and flour.

Optional: Use another piece of paper to rewrite the passage without errors.

Read the passage and correct the agreement errors. There are no errors in the picture or caption.

## 50. The Treasure Hunters

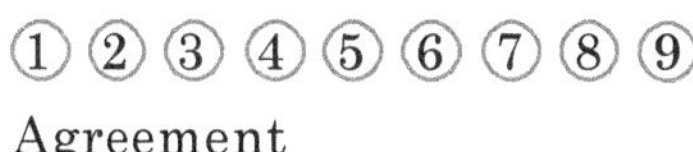


Agreement

Carmen and Yoko had just read the story "The Treasure Hunters" in the best-selling book *Secrets of Lost Treasures.* These morning, she wanted to play the board game with Anna and me. "We'll play," I said, "if you gives us a head start of five squares."

"Well, okay," Carmen conceded. "Who's ready to start?" Even though we had a 5-square head start, by 9:00 a.m. Carmen and Yoko had gotten our scuba gear, passed the danger zones, and landed two moves from the treasure chest entrance. Things wasn't looking too good for us. It would have taken more than luck for us to get out of Big Brig and swipe the goods. Anna and I lost the game just as we expected. Some of the games we play is just easier to win than others. These game was clearly their worst game ever. Oh well, I guess you wins some and you lose some!

GAME PIECES

Carmen and Yoko - 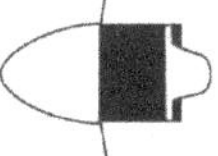

Anna and Cheryl - 

9:00 a.m.: Even though Anna and Cheryl had a 5-square head start, things are looking bad for them as they wait hopelessly in the brig (jail).

Optional: Use another piece of paper to rewrite the passage without errors.

Read the passage and correct the agreement errors. There are no errors in the picture or caption.

## 51. Armchair Adventure

①②③④⑤⑥⑦⑧
Agreement

"Did you knows that a geyser is like a pot bubbling over on the stove?" Brandon asked her sister. "Boiling water expands into steam, and the water and steam explodes out of the geyser's mouth. It says here that minerals in the water forms cones or even towers around the mouth of a geyser."

"I already know all that," said Becky, "because his aunt has been to Yellowstone National Park, Wyoming, with their husband."

"She went with whom?" interrupted Brandon.

"She went with Uncle Earl," Becky answered impatiently, "and they also went to New Zealand and saw geysers right from their hotel room."

"Wow!" said Brandon. "Maybe they'll take you and me next time."

Brandon hoped to see the sights shown in the magazine he were reading. How about you? Would you likes to see the places in "Hot Spots: Great Geysers of the World?"

The article that Brandon is reading in *Adventure Travel* shows pictures from three areas in the world in which you can see geysers: Yellowstone National Park in Wyoming, Rotorua on the north island of New Zealand, and a site near Reykjavik, Iceland.

Optional: Use another piece of paper to rewrite the passage without errors.

Read the passage and correct the agreement errors. There are no errors in the picture or caption.

## 52. On the Loose

① ② ③ ④ ⑤ ⑥ ⑦ ⑧ ⑨ ⑩ Agreement

It was an exciting day when this tiger escaped from a derailed train bound for the zoo and ended up in someone's backyard!

Emmet Levison, zookeeper, recall the days of transporting animals by train. They reminisces about one day in particular that turned out to be a very exciting one. "Once, a train carrying a shipment of ours derailed and let thirty animals go free. Most of the beasts was rounded up, but an elusive tiger had fled to a nearby backyard. After he were tranquilized, the big cat slumped into a patch of berries and could not even rise onto his feet." Emmet added that none of those animals was injured or lost, but that the zoo administrator and she was worried. Emmet remember saying, "Now that these animals has tasted freedom, we can't be sure I could recapture them if this should ever happen again."

Optional: Use another piece of paper to rewrite the passage without errors.

# Lesson 11. Confused Words/Negative Words

A. **Confused Words**

**Confused words** may or may not sound alike. They have different spellings and meanings.

Below is a list of confused words, their meanings, and examples of how to use them correctly.

1. **Accept** is a verb that means to receive. ......... Janis will **accept** the prize for winning.
   **Except** is a preposition/conjunction that means to leave out. .............................. Everyone got a prize **except** Richard.

2. **Affect** is a verb that means to influence. ......... Lots of sleep can **affect** your grades.
   **Effect** is a noun that means a result. ............. Your final grades were the **effect** of lots of sleep.

3. **Bring** is a verb that means to carry something here. ............................................. **Bring** the cake to the birthday party.
   **Take** is a verb that means to carry something there. .......................................... Jasmine will **take** the book home.

4. **Farther** is an adverb that refers to length or distance.......................................... The gas station is **farther** from the shop than my house.
   **Further** is an adverb that refers to time, degree, or quantity. .............................. We can discuss this **further** on Friday.

5. **Lie** is a verb that means to rest or recline. ..... When I watch TV, I **lie** on the couch.
   **Lay** is a verb that means to put or place something. ................................ Mason will **lay** the computer on the desk.

6. **Less** is an adjective used when you cannot count it. .......................................... Saphron has **less** homework than I do.
   **Fewer** is an adjective when you can count it. ................................................ Brianna ate **fewer** chips than Jose did.

7. **Leave** is a verb that means to go away. ........... Please **leave** my brother alone.
   **Let** is a verb that means to allow. .................... I will **let** you pet the huge snake.

8. **Lose** is a verb that means to not win. ............. The jackal will **lose** his fight to the lion.
   **Loose** is an adjective that means not tight. ..... The chain is **loose** on the bicycle.

9. **May** is a verb that means to be permitted. ...... **May** I open the package for you?
   **Can** is a verb that means to be able to. ........... I **can** solve the math problem quickly.

10. **Precede** is a verb that means to come before. ............ Saturday will **precede** Sunday.
    **Proceed** is a verb that means to continue. ............ The snake will **proceed** toward the mouse.

11. **Quiet** is an adjective that means little or no noise. ............ The classroom is not **quiet** when people are talking.
    **Quit** is a verb that means to stop. ............ Please **quit** hitting the desk with your hand.
    **Quite** is an adverb that means truly or considerably. ............ The painting is **quite** exquisite.

12. **Raise** is a verb that means something moves something else to a higher position, to elevate. ............ The crane will **raise** the bricks up higher.
    **Rise** is a verb that means something moves from lower to higher. ............ The hot air balloon will **rise** into the air.

13. **Then** is an adverb that refers to time. ............ My mom will pick me up and **then** take me to my tennis lesson.
    **Than** is a conjunction used only to compare ............ Erica understands algebra better **than** her older sister.

14. **Teach** is a verb that means to instruct. ............ I will **teach** the class to dance.
    **Learn** is a verb that means to gain knowledge or understanding. ............ Today we will start to **learn** French.

B. **Negative Words**

1. Use only one **negative** word to state a negative idea. ............ Incorrect: We **don't** have **no** dessert.
   Correct: We **don't** have any dessert.
   Correct: We have **no** dessert.

2. The words ***hardly*** and ***scarcely*** are also considered negative words and should not be used with other negatives. ............ Incorrect: We have **hardly no** dessert.
   Correct: We have **hardly** any dessert.
   Correct: We have **no** dessert.

 

Read the passage and correct the confused word pair/negative words errors. There are no errors in the picture or caption.

## 53. Bales of Fun

①②③④⑤⑥⑦⑧⑨
Confused Word
①
Negative Word

Rural Route 1

Canton, NY 13617

June 11, 2010

Dear Pham,

I'll bet your city is very exciting, but believe me, living in rural St. Lawrence County may be great. We are located northwest of Lake Ontario between the Adirondack Mountains and Canada. My sister and I work here on a dairy farm and teach something every day from our chores. At milking time, I spread the straw while Cindy takes pails of milk to me in the barn. When we do the haying, Cindy picks up bales weighing a hundred pounds each and will lie them onto the wagon. She just doesn't quiet! While drinking iced tea, I drive the tractor pulling the wagon. Than at the barn, I watch the bales raise to the loft on the hay elevator. I leave Cindy have the honor of catching and neatly stacking the bales in the 100° heat of the barn. The affect is it's a great life for her and me! I don't understand why Cindy can't not wait to go to college in the city.

Sincerely,

Manuel

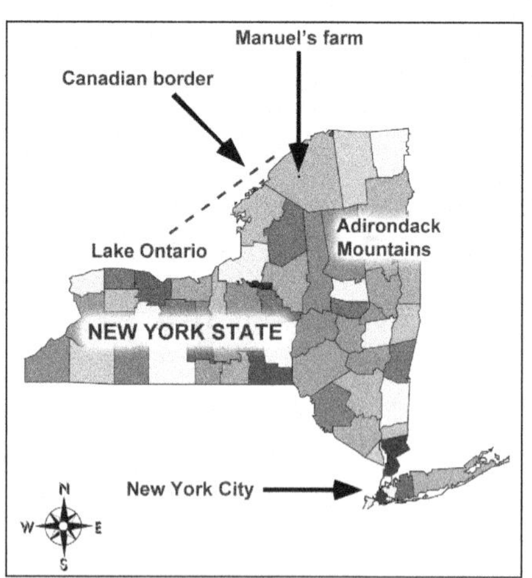

Manuel's farm is in the largest county of the state of New York.

Optional: Use another piece of paper to rewrite the passage without errors.

Read the passage and correct the confused word pair/negative words errors. There are no errors in the picture or caption.

## 54. How to Catch a Wave

①②③④⑤⑥⑦⑧⑨
Confused Word
①
Negative Word

The first steps in teaching how to surf are balancing on the surfboard and paddling. To begin, lay horizontally along the center of the board. To balance, place your feet close together on the board. Paddling is done with alternating left and right strokes. After you have paddled out, you should than face the ocean and start looking for a wave that is further out. When you see a good wave, turn yourself and your board toward the beach and begin paddling as strong and fast as you may. Arch your back to keep the nose of your board from going underwater, and the wave will give you a nice push. When you can except the force of the wave, you should rise yourself up and place your feet sideways on the board. Keep your board quiet steady and just ahead of the breaking wave. Your knees should be bent, and your torso should be slightly forward. Now hang lose, and don't not wipe out!

Remember, your feet and legs should be close together while paddling in order to balance the board. While surfing the wave, keep your knees bent and your torso slightly forward.

Optional: Use another piece of paper to rewrite the passage without errors.

Read the passage and correct the confused word pair/negative words errors. There are no errors in the picture or caption.

## 55. Schedule It!

①②③④⑤⑥⑦⑧
Confused Word
①②
Negative Word

Did she like being disorganized? Did she enjoy doing homework when her friends asked, "May you go dancing?" No, she didn't hardly. On the other hand, she felt quit overwhelmed with things to do. I have not hardly any time!

Her father, who was a good advisor, came to the rescue with an article called "Doing It All." He said, "Prioritize your activities, and then leave go of the things that matter the least. Schedule important things first, and fit the other stuff around them. Except it and you'll get further."

Than, Juanita began penciling activities on her schedule. She managed to include at least one fun thing each day. On Thursdays, she would surf at 3:30 and precede to watch her favorite television show at 9:30. Instead of playing with her brother after doing dishes, she may practice her music for 45 minutes. She was pleased as she closed her eyes that night. "Tomorrow," Juanita said, "things will be different!"

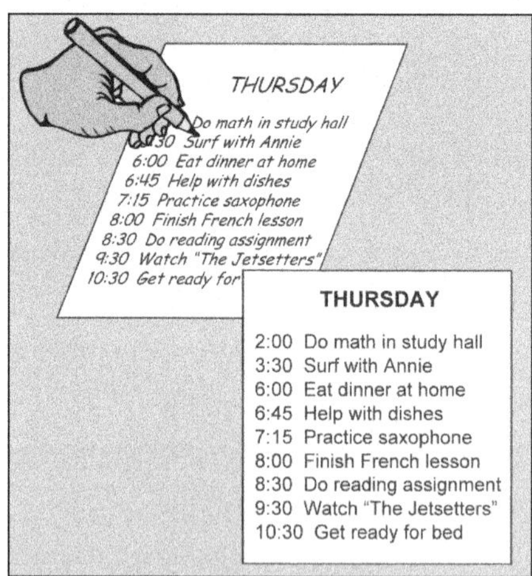


The above picture shows both Juanita's penciled version and her final printout of the schedule for Thursdays.

Optional: Use another piece of paper to rewrite the passage without errors.

Read the passage and correct the confused word pair/negative words errors. There are no errors in the picture or caption.

## 56. Stained Glass

① ② ③ ④ ⑤ ⑥ ⑦ ⑧ ⑨
Confused Word
①
Negative Word

As visitors to a prominent window maker, we are honored to be given a tour by the owner. "At Stained Panes, Inc.," President Cutler explains, "the art of constructing stained glass windows has been carefully preserved. The affect of our final products is great because they are made with special glass imported from Europe. We learn students to cut plain glass first. Would you like to watch one of our apprentices?" We look on as he says to the student, "For now, you may make a straight cut. You must lie the glass cutter down and apply pressure as you roll it along a straight guide to the end then quiet. Precede using the glass pliers to separate the two pieces of glass. Finally, rise the piece to see how you've done." Than Mr. Cutler says, "Next time, we'll try some curves. Stained glass isn't hardly an easy craft to perfect, but you will know it is worthwhile when you see the sun raise through a window of red and gold German glass."

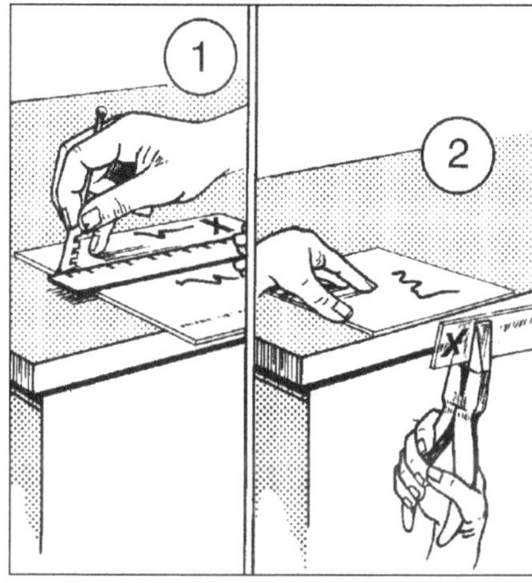


The student cuts a strip of glass. (1) She uses a glass cutter to make a straight score, or scratch. (2) She carefully separates the strip from the glass sheet by using a pair of glass pliers.

Optional: Use another piece of paper to rewrite the passage without errors.

 

## Lesson 12. Run-On Sentences and Sentence Fragments

A **sentence** is a group of words that form a complete thought. A complete sentence always contains a subject (noun or pronoun) and a predicate (verb). The subject tells who or what the sentence is about. The predicate tells what is happening.

A. There are two types of run-on sentences.

1. A **run-on sentence** contains two or more complete sentences that should be separate sentences.

    Shayna loves peas she hates broccoli.

    To correct a run-on sentence, follow these steps:
    1. Put a period after the first complete sentence.
    2. Capitalize the first word of the new sentence.

    Shayna loves peas. She hates broccoli.

2. A **run-on sentence** can also be caused by using the word **and** to join two or more ideas that should be separate. As you read the example, think about where one idea ends and another begins.

    We all went to the park yesterday **and** the boys played volleyball **and** the girls swam in the lake.

    a. The run-on sentence above has three ideas joined by "and." To correct it, make three separate sentences.
        1. Delete every *and* that is not needed.
        2. Put a period in place of each unnecessary *and.*
        3. Capitalize the first word in each new sentence.

    We all went to the park yesterday. The boys played volleyball. The girls swam in the lake.

    b. You can also make two sentences if two of the ideas are closely related. You can:
        1. Use a comma before the conjunction *and* to combine the two closely related ideas.

    We all went to the park yesterday. The boys played volleyball, *and* the girls swam in the lake.

        2. Use a *subordinating conjunction* to join the two sentences.

    We all went to the park yesterday. The boys played volleyball *while* the girls swam in the lake.

3. Use a semicolon between the two complete sentences.

We all went to the park yesterday; the boys played volleyball. The girls swam in the lake.

B. A **sentence fragment** is only part of a sentence. It can be missing a subject (noun or pronoun), a predicate (verb), a subject and a predicate, or just be an incomplete thought.

1. Below is a sentence fragment. It needs to be rewritten to make a complete sentence.

A bird on the fence. (lacks a predicate; incomplete thought)

To make a complete sentence, add a **predicate** to the fragment.

A bird on the fence chirped merrily. (complete sentence)

2. Below is another sentence fragment. It needs to be rewritten to make a complete sentence.

Missed the bus. (lacks a subject; incomplete thought)

To make a complete sentence, add a **subject** to the fragment.

**Reuben** missed the bus. (complete sentence)
**He** missed the bus. (complete sentence)

3. Below are two sentence fragments. They need to be rewritten to make a complete sentence.

The kindergarten teacher. (lacks a predicate; incomplete thought)
Read a story to the class. (lacks a subject; incomplete thought)

To make a complete sentence, remove the period after *teacher* and change the capital **R** to lower case.

The kindergarten **teacher read** a story to the class. (complete sentence)

Read the passage and correct the run-on sentence and sentence fragment errors. There are no errors in the picture or caption.

## 57. The Burning Phoenix

① ② ③ ④ ⑤
Run-On Sentence
① ② ③ ④ ⑤
Sentence Fragment

The phoenix existed in Greek mythology and was said to live for five hundred years. At the end of the phoenix's life cycle, he would build a fire and burn himself. A new phoenix would arise from the ashes.

The phoenix was a bird in Greek and Egyptian mythology and it was as large or larger than an eagle and had brilliant scarlet and gold plumage and it had a melodious cry. Only one. Phoenix existed at any time, and it was always male and the Greek and Egyptian writers said he lived to be. Five hundred years old. When the life cycle of the phoenix. Came to a close, he would gather wood and other burnable items and light himself on fire out of the ashes, a new phoenix would arise. The new phoenix would then carry. The ashes of his father to the sun god, Re, in Heliopolis (City of the Sun). Because of the long life span of the phoenix and his rebirth from the ashes, he symbolized. Immortality and rebirth and he was also said to symbolize the rising and setting of the sun.

Optional: Use another piece of paper to rewrite the passage without errors.

Read the passage and correct the run-on sentence and sentence fragment errors. There are no errors in the picture or caption.

## 58. Uses of Peanut Oil

① ② ③ ④ ⑤ ⑥
Run-On Sentence
① ② ③ ④
Sentence Fragment

Watch out if you have just eaten a peanut butter sandwich that snack of yours might be. More powerful than you think. The oil of peanuts is used for making nitroglycerin, an explosive ingredient of dynamite and peanut oil is also commonly used in household items. It can be used. To make soap by the process of saponification. It is safe for use as a massage oil and in fact, in 1933, noted peanut researcher George Washington Carver developed. A peanut massage oil to treat polio. At the 1900 Paris Exhibition, the Otto Company, at the request of the French government, demonstrated that peanut oil could be used as a source of fuel for the diesel engine and this was one of the earliest demonstrations of bio-diesel technology. Grooming products and paint sometimes. Contain peanut oil. It is used in salad dressing, too and compared to olive oil, peanut oil is considered by some people to be tastier and indeed, peanut oil has many uses.

Peanut oil is a common ingredient in many household items, including paint, grooming products, and salad dressing. It is also used to make nitroglycerin, the principal explosive ingredient of dynamite!

Optional: Use another piece of paper to rewrite the passage without errors.

Read the passage and correct the run-on sentence and sentence fragment errors. There are no errors in the picture or caption.

## 59. Ride the Wild River

① ② ③ ④
Run-On Sentence
① ② ③ ④ ⑤ ⑥
Sentence Fragment

Robert's Roaring Rapids River Tours offer several packages. A guide is provided on each raft, and no experience is required.

Rafting is a sport that appeals. To the adventurous athlete. It's like a roller coaster ride without the seat belts and the beginning of our journey downriver was calm and uneventful. We entered the rapids more abruptly. Than I had expected. The raft was lifted by a wave and dropped into a pool of swirling water and the raft spun around several times before the guide could point it back downriver. Our paddles were. Useless in the rushing water. We spent the rest of our time. Bailing out all 13 feet of our raft as wave after wave came pouring over us and we were so wet and chilly that we were shaking as we finally. Pulled into shore for the night and what an exhilarating day we'd had! Would we do it again if. We had the chance? You bet we would!

Optional: Use another piece of paper to rewrite the passage without errors.

Read the passage and correct the run-on sentence and sentence fragment errors. There are no errors in the picture or caption.

## 60. Birth of a Volcano

① ② ③ ④ ⑤ ⑥
Run-On Sentence
① ② ③ ④
Sentence Fragment

Imagine that you are walking through a cornfield and the day is fine, but you are a bit nervous because there have been a lot of earthquakes lately and suddenly, a crack opens in the ground and comes racing. Toward you. Steam and sulfur gas rise from the crack and carry. The smell of rotten eggs. You run away and half an hour later you hear an explosion and see a black cloud rising high into the air and these events could have happened to you if you had been. Walking in the corn field 180 miles west of Mexico City, Mexico, on February 20, 1943, when the volcano Paricutin was born. Three weeks before the eruption actually occurred, rumbling noises that resembled thunder. Were heard by people near Paricutin Village and these were actually deep earthquakes. Like most cinder cone volcanoes, Paricutin is believed to be a monogenetic volcano, which means that once it has finished erupting it well never erupt again in 1952, Paricutin finished erupting and has been quiet ever since.

The volcano Parícutin was born in a corn field 180 miles west of Mexico City on the 20th day of the second month of 1943. The eruption started with a crack opening and spewing forth steam and sulfur gas, which smelled like rotten eggs.

Optional: Use another piece of paper to rewrite the passage without errors.

 

# Mini Review

# Lessons 10–12

Read the passage and correct the errors. There are no errors in the picture or caption.

## 61. Print Patterns

| | |
|---|---|
| ① ② | Agreement |
| ① ② ③ | Confused Word |
| ① | Negative Word |
| ① ② | Run-On Sentence |
| ① ② | Sentence Fragment |

Have you ever heard that hardly no two fingerprints are alike? Everyone has different fingerprint patterns. That fingerprints are made up of a pattern of ridges that vary. In number, size, and location. There are three basic patterns of fingerprints: loops, whorls, and arches. The most commonly occurring of the three patterns are the loop a loop must have one ridge that enters from one side, curves around, and exits from the same side. Whorls involve ridges. That curve in a circular pattern. The arch, the least common pattern, is formed by ridges that enter from one side, raise in the middle, and than exit. A print from the foot may also leave an impression with ridges be careful what you touch or where you walk!

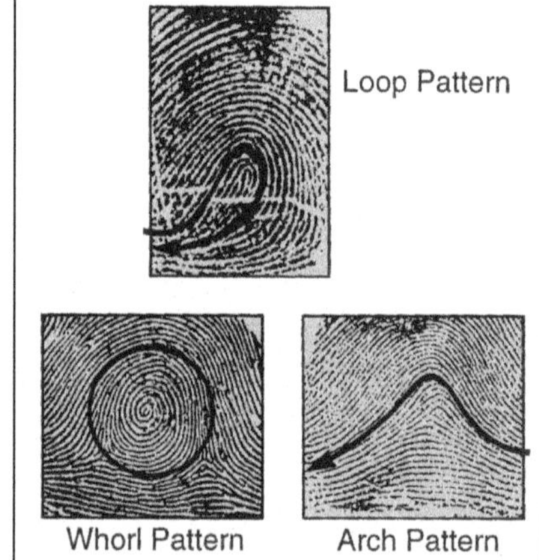


The three types of fingerprint patterns are the loop, the whorl, and the arch. The most common pattern, the loop, has a ridge that enters and exits from the same side.

Optional: Use another piece of paper to rewrite the passage without errors.

Read the passage and correct the errors. There are no errors in the picture or caption.

## 62. The Monkey in the Jeep

| | |
|---|---|
| ①②③④ | Agreement |
| ①②③④ | Confused Word |
| ①② | Run-On Sentence |
| ①② | Sentence Fragment |

The monkey kept racing in and out of the jeep to take whatever he could find.

You never know what will happen in the savannahs of Eastern Africa. In the country of Tanzania, a caravan of tired travelers came. Upon a place to rest and take a break. Everyone wanted to go see the herd of elephants who were close by, accept two of the travelers who stayed behind. They began to watch a small monkey walking toward the jeep. In a split second, those monkey preceded to take off running, and jumped in the jeep he than grabbed the closest drink box and scampered up the nearest tree. Few travelers were so surprised, yet excited, because they had been taking pictures the entire time the monkey. Was racing in and out of the jeep. Soon none the travelers returned only to teach that they had missed out this had been a once in a lifetime experience for the two travelers and the monkey in the jeep!

Optional: Use another piece of paper to rewrite the passage without errors.

# Review
# Lessons 7–12

Read the passage and correct the errors. There are no errors in the picture or caption.

## 63. Mammal Discovery

| | |
|---|---|
| ① ② | Pronoun |
| ① ② | Verb |
| ① | Clause/Phrase |
| ① ② ③ ④ | Agreement |
| ① | Confused Word |
| ① | Run-On Sentence |
| ① | Sentence Fragment |

In the early 1990s scientists discover two new species of mammals. Both was found in the isolated and mountainous Vu Quang Nature Reserve in Vietnam. The Vu Quang ox, also known as a saola or Asian unicorn, are an ox that has long horns and a dark brown coat with a black stripe along it's back. It weighs about 220 pounds. It is a distant relative to sheep and cattle and it was the first new large mammal found in more than 50 years. It is a forest-dwelling bovine and one. Of the world's rarest mammals. The giant muntjac, a deer with huge canine teeth, was discovered soon after the Vu Quange ox. It have a reddish brown coat and weigh between 66 and 110 pounds. The first live specimen caught it was a Vu Quang ox calf. It was sent to a botanical garden in Hanoi for study. The affect of hunting, combined with slash and burn agriculture, have caused the giant muntjac to be considered an endangered species. It is also preyed upon by animals such as the tiger and the leopard.

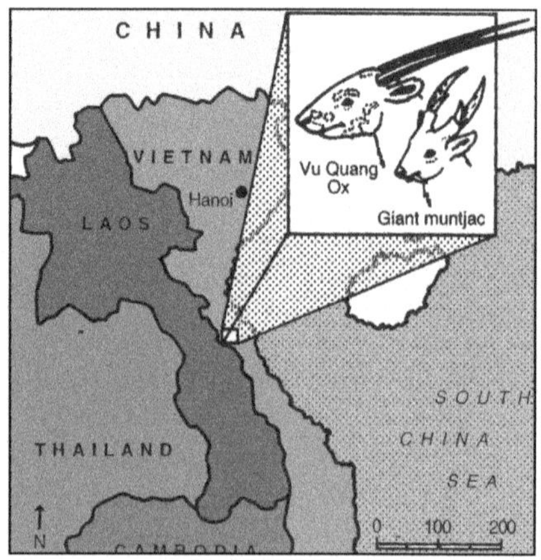


The first new large mammals discovered in over 50 years, the Vu Quang ox and the giant muntjac, were discovered in the Vu Quang Nature Reserve (see box in picture) in the 1990s.

Optional: Use another piece of paper to rewrite the passage without errors.

Read the passage and correct the errors. There are no errors in the picture or caption.

## 64. Victory on Wheels

| | |
|---|---|
| ① | Pronoun |
| ① ② | Verb |
| ① ② | Clause/Phrase |
| ① ② | Agreement |
| ① | Confused Word |
| ① | Negative Word |
| ① | Run-On Sentence |
| ① ② | Sentence Fragment |

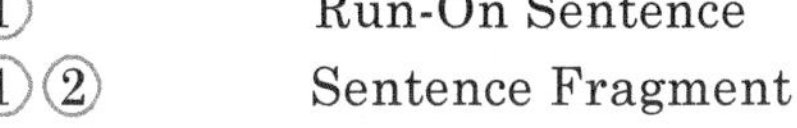

Amy was fast that day. In fact, she had hardly never ridden faster. “She rides like the wind,” her husband said as she whizzed by. She been leading the pack by more than 30 seconds. She thrust her fists in the air and yelled excitedly as she came across the finish line twenty-two seconds before the next finisher. It was her second victory. In a bicycle race.

On the way home she and her husband tried to decide what contributed to her great finish. “Was it what I ate?” she ask.

“Maybe it were because you were well rested,” he guessed.

They decided that. Her success was probably a combination of all the possibilities, and that made it difficult to duplicate and anyway, victory was her’s. Looking to the future Amy’s mind was already racing to the women’s triathlon that would take place in three weeks. May she make it his next victory?

Amy was in the lead for the entire 20-mile competition. She cruised to a first-place finish in 48 minutes, 45 seconds. She was just catching her breath when the next finisher came in at 49 minutes, 7 seconds.

Optional: Use another piece of paper to rewrite the passage without errors.

Read the passage and correct the errors. There are no errors in the picture or caption.

## 65. Count on Computers

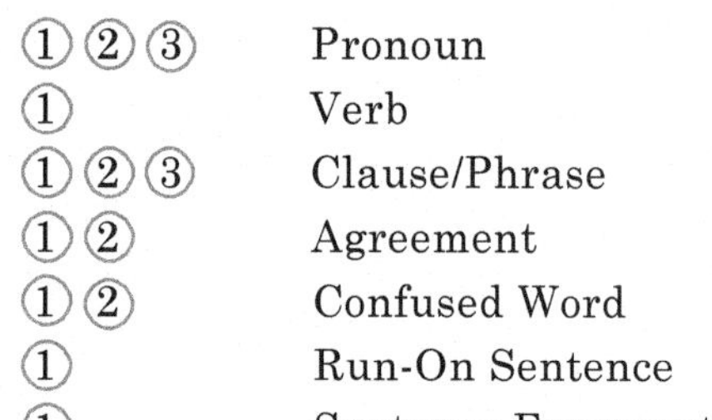

| | |
|---|---|
| ① ② ③ | Pronoun |
| ① | Verb |
| ① ② ③ | Clause/Phrase |
| ① ② | Agreement |
| ① ② | Confused Word |
| ① | Run-On Sentence |
| ① | Sentence Fragment |

We humans like to make things easy for us. Because we have eight fingers and two thumbs we use the decimal number system. It is based on ten digits. Computers, however, are more suited to the binary, or base two, system and base two requires only two symbols. A one or a zero can easily in the computer be expressed as either a flow of electricity or no flow of electricity. How do we. Read a number in base two? On the farthest right is the ones place. The next place to the left are the twos place. The third place shows how many fours, the fourth place shows how many eights, and so on. Than we add all the values who hold ones to get the equivalent decimal number. Therefore, the binary number in the illustration represent our decimal number twenty-one. Since only two states of electric flow need to be used the binary number system lets computers process information more easily then they could otherwise. Computers, in turn, can made things easier for ourselves. Awesome!

Two different numbers are shown, a decimal number on the upper right and a binary number below. The binary number system uses the symbols 1 and 0. For each 1, add the decimal value of its place (shown below the blank). This binary number represents the sum of 1, 4, and 16.

Optional: Use another piece of paper to rewrite the passage without errors.

Read the passage and correct the errors. There are no errors in the picture or caption.

## 66. An Archaeological Find

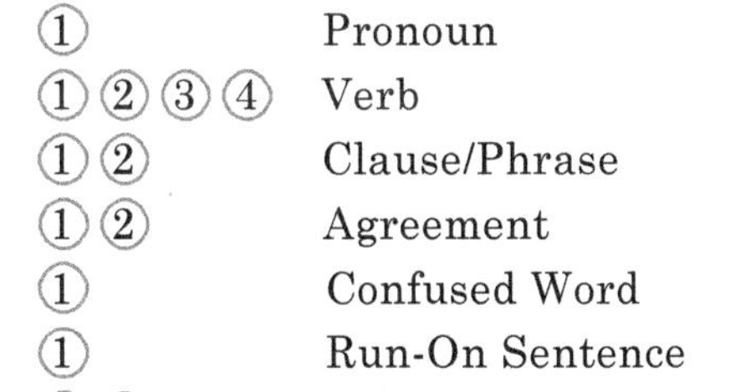


Today, our exacting field work in Australia was reward. We spended most of the day carefully uncovering what seemed to be an ancient knife. We had many questions and when was it made? Was it used as a weapon? Was it. Used for cooking? Once the knife uncovered, we noticed another object just below it. He was a small wood carving in the shape of a dingo, a dog brought to Australia by the Aborigines about 5,000 to 8,000 years ago. We theorized that the knife. Was most likely used to carve the wooden dog. However, we had no indication of the carving's age. We will had to use the tree ring dating method to find out how old the carving actually is. Every wooden object have tree rings. Each ring represents one year. Of growth. We will compare the rings of the carving to the rings of a nearby tree to see where they match. He are eager to really find out how old these artifacts are. What more will we teach?

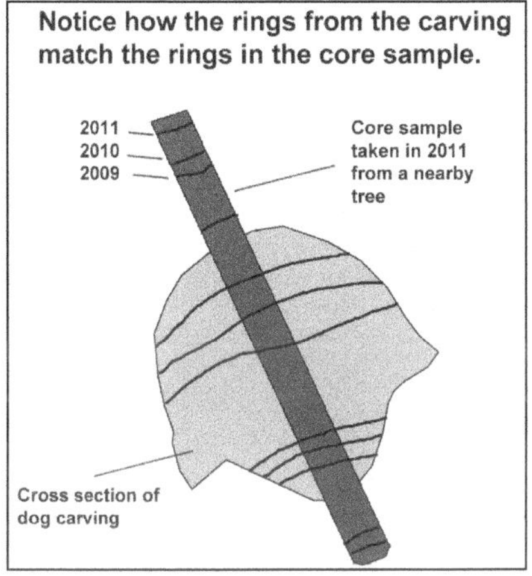


The core sample is laid on a cross section of the carving to see where the rings match. Since the age of the core sample is known, the scientists can count backward the number of rings (years) to see how old the artifact is. The carving turns out to be quite new!

Optional: Use another piece of paper to rewrite the passage without errors.

# Final Review
# Lessons 1–12

Read the passage and correct the errors. There are no errors in the picture or caption.

## 67. Close Call

| | |
|---|---|
| ① ② | Content |
| ① | Punctuation |
| ① ② ③ | Spelling |
| ① | Preposition |
| ① | Adjective |
| ① | Adverb |
| ① ② | Verb |
| ① | Negative Word |
| ① | Run-On Sentence |
| ① | Clause |

The day got off to a great start! It was springtime and the weather was perfect. So, Dakota and his wife Catori, decided to pack up the family into their convirtible and go for a Saturday afternoon drive in the forest. They were enjoying the beautiful scenery along Forest Way, while listening to the tune Wild Nature. Sudden, two deer appeared out of nowhere. In order to avoid hitting the deer Dakota ran the car into in a maple tree. Fortunately, no won was hurt! Dakota exclaim, “Wow! I’ve hardly never saw animals appear so suddenly.” It was a little scary for everyone since it happened so unexpectedly and the doe and the fawn were the beautiful deers they’d ever seen. They’ll most likely never encounter those two again, but they’ll sure have a beauty of a dent to remind them of those deer.

A driver hit a pine tree after swerving to avoid a doe and her fawn crossing Forest Drive.

Optional: Use another piece of paper to rewrite the passage without errors.

Read the passage and correct the errors. There are no errors in the picture or caption.

# 68. An Educational Trip

| | |
|---|---|
| ①②③ | Content |
| ① | Capitalization |
| ①② | Punctuation |
| ①② | Spelling |
| ① | Conjunction |
| ①② | Pronoun |
| ① | Agreement |
| ① | Confused Word |
| ① | Sentence Fragment |

529 Evergreen Court

Boise, ID 83704

July 8, 2007

Dear Hiroshi!

My parents took my brother and myself to the seashore. Either my brother nor I had ever seen the ocean before. Wow It was really great. There was seagulls all around the shore. We saw alot of plants and animals in the water, too. Did you. Know that there are many kinds of seaweeds? Seaweeds can be brown, red, or green. They are all algae, and they attach themself to rocks. The part attached to the sand is called a holdtight, and small animals live in it. Animals live on the leaves, to. One type of seaweed can grow a foot in a day, and some seaweeds grow to be very long. We saw a giant kelp that was green and almost 200 feet long! This trip sure did learn us a lot!

sincerely,

Basha

The rocky shore is home to many animals. It is also home to many kinds of seaweeds. Seaweeds can be brown, red, or green algae. Seaweeds attach themselves to rocks with a holdfast. Green algae do not grow as large as brown and red algae do. Giant kelp, a brown algae, can grow to be 200 feet long.

Optional: Use another piece of paper to rewrite the passage without errors.

Read the passage and correct the errors. There are no errors in the picture or caption.

## 69. Pangolins

| | |
|---|---|
| ① ② | Content |
| ① | Capitalization |
| ① ② | Punctuation |
| ① ② ③ | Spelling |
| ① | Article |
| ① | Verb |
| ① | Clause/Phrase |
| ① | Agreement |
| ① | Run-On Sentence |
| ① | Sentence Fragment |

There are an total of eight species of pangolin on our planet. Four of them live in Asia, and the other four live in Africa. Pangolins, also known as scaly anteaters, are unique creatures that are cover in hard, overlapping scales and they are insectiverous feeding on insects and are mainly nocturnal. Their name is derived from the malay word "pengguling," which loosely translates to "something that rolls up." They have large, dull claws that they use for excavating ant and termite nests, and also for pulling bark off trees and logs to locate their insect prey. Pangolins don't have teeth and are unable to chew. Instead, they have short, sticky tongues that they use to catch the insects they feed on. When a pangolin's tongue is fully extended they can be up to 16 inches longer than its entire body length. It is believeed that a single pangolin. Consumes more than 70 million insects per year. A pangolins diet consists mainly of ants and termites. Pangolin's have poor vision and hearing, but an excellent sense of smell.

The pangolin has:
1. large, sharp claws
2. no teeth
3. a long, sticky tongue
4. poor vision and hearing
5. good sense of smell

Optional: Use another piece of paper to rewrite the passage without errors.

# Answers

**1. On a Grand Scale** (p. 2)

The ancient Egyptian architects built on a grand scale. Their greatest achievement was the pyramids. In comparison to modern structures, the pyramids were relatively **short**[1] in height but **massive**[2] in volume. These pyramids were constructed as tombs for the pharaohs. The base of the Great Pyramid near Cairo lies on a piece of land equal in size to **ten**[3] football fields. Huge **limestone**[4] blocks weighing as much as **5,000**[5] pounds were placed layer upon layer to raise pyramids that were around **500**[6] feet tall. Egyptian architects also built their structures to last. The **three**[7] pyramids at Giza are the largest and best preserved of all the **Egyptian**[8] pyramids. They're over **4,000**[9] years old. The pyramids are considered one of the Seven Wonders of the Ancient World and are the only ones still standing.

1. short – Content: See caption.
2. massive – Content: See caption.
3. ten – Content: See caption.
4. limestone – Content: See caption.
5. 5,000 pounds – Content: See caption.
6. 500 feet – Content: See picture.
7. three – Content: See caption.
8. Egyptian – Content: See caption.
9. 4,000 years – Content: See caption.

**2. Time for Fun** (p. 3)

We plan to see all the shows while we are at Fun Park, **Idaho**[1]. We notice on the schedule that the Wild Animal Show will take place at **12:00**[2] p.m. and 3:00 p.m. The Bird Show is in the **small**[3] arena next to the **Wild Animal Show**[4] and will be presented at 10:00 a.m. and 2:00 p.m. We really want to see the Wild West Stunt Show on the other side of the park. We can see the animal show at 12:00 p.m. in the **large**[5] arena if we go to the Bird Show at 10:00 a.m. Then we can take a break for lunch and go to the stunt show at **1:00**[6] p.m. **on the stage**[7]. Or, in the morning we can see the **Bird**[8] Show first, the **stunt**[9] show next, and the animal show in the afternoon. Anyway, we will have seen them all by the day's end.

1. Idaho – Content: See caption.
2. 12:00 p.m. – Content: See picture.
3. small – Content: See picture
4. Wild Animal Show or large arena – Content: See picture.
5. large – Content: See picture.
6. 1:00 p.m. – Content: See picture.
7. on the ~~small~~ stage – Content: See picture.
8. Bird – Content: See picture.
9. stunt – Content: See picture.

**3. Venus Flytrap** (p. 4)

Deep in the bogs of coastal North and South **Carolina**[1] lurks an unusual plant, the Venus flytrap. The bogs provide **damp**[2] soil, but the soil lacks the **nitrogen**[3] that the plant needs to survive. The Venus flytrap has developed a unique way of acquiring this essential nutrient. Its **rounded**[4], hinged leaves have **bristled**[5] edges and sensitive hairs on the inside. When prey touches the hairs, the leaf closes quickly. The struggling victim is trapped as the plant **secretes**[6] fluids to digest the insect and receive the needed nitrogen. Most **carnivorous**[7] plants selectively feed on specific prey. This selection is based on the available prey and the type of trap used by the organism. With the Venus flytrap, prey is limited to **beetles**[8], spiders, and other crawling arthropods. Unfortunately, the Venus flytrap is currently considered to be a **vulnerable**[9] and threatened species due to over-collection, habitat destruction, and fire suppression.

1. Carolina – Content: See caption.
2. damp – Content: See caption.
3. nitrogen – Content: See caption.
4. rounded – Content: See caption.
5. bristled – Content: See caption.
6. secretes – Content: See caption.
7. carnivorous – Content: See caption.
8. beetles – Content: See caption.
9. vulnerable – Content: See caption.

**4. Spiders and Crabs** (p. 5)

Spiders and crabs can look very similar and are, in fact, both classified as arthropods. Arthropods are **invertebrate**[1] animals that have jointed legs and segmented bodies. Both a spider and a crab have **two**[2] main body sections: the cephalothorax **and**[3] the abdomen. The cephalothorax is a combined head and chest to which the legs are attached. The spider has **eight**[4] legs, and the crab has **ten**[5]. All arthropods also have **outer**[6] shells called exoskeletons that protect and support their bodies, improve locomotion, and shed periodically as they grow. Crabs have compound eyes that consist of **many**[7] lenses, but spiders' eyes have only one lens each. Unlike other types of arthropods, spiders have no antennae. However, crabs usually have two pairs of antennae on their **heads**[8]. The crabs use these antennae as **sense**[9] organs.

1. invertebrate – Content: See caption.
2. two – Content: See picture.
3. and the abdomen. – Content: See picture.
4. eight – Content: See picture.
5. ten – Content: See picture.
6. outer – Content: See caption.
7. many – Content: See caption.
8. heads – Content: See picture.
9. sense – Content: See caption.

**5. A Foot in the Door** (p. 8)

1555 Revolution **Road**[1]
San Diego, **CA**[2] 92115
**June**[3] 11, 2013

**Dr.**[4] Emelda Walsh
Community Hospital of San Francisco
**San**[5] Francisco, CA 94150

**Dear**[6] Dr. Walsh:

As a recent graduate in the field of medicine, **I**[7] was pleased to see an opening for a medical technician at your hospital.

**My**[8] experience in the field of health began in 2004 when I was a volunteer for the children's cancer ward at **Grossmont**[9] Hospital. For the last six years, I have been working as a medical technician in **Southern**[10] California for the San Diego **Hospital**[11].

I recognize and greatly admire the work that the Community Hospital of San Francisco has been doing since its start in 1908. I look forward to speaking with you regarding my qualifications.

**Sincerely**[12],
Antonio Brainsworthy

1. Road – Capitalization: Capitalize the name of a road.
2. CA – Capitalization: Capitalize the name of a state.
3. June – Capitalization: Capitalize a month of the year.
4. Dr. – Capitalization: Capitalize a person's title and its abbreviation.
5. San – Capitalization: Capitalize the name of a city.
6. Dear – Capitalization: Capitalize the first word in the greeting of a letter.
7. I – Capitalization: Capitalize the pronoun I.
8. My – Capitalization: Capitalize the first word of a sentence.
9. Grossmont – Capitalization: Capitalize the name of a place.
10. Southern – Capitalization: Capitalize compass points when they represent specific regions.
11. Hospital – Capitalization: Capitalize the name of a place.
12. Sincerely – Capitalization: Capitalize the first word in the closing in a letter.

**6. Earth Day Celebration** (p. 9)

**The**[1] first Earth Day was celebrated on **April**[2] 22, 1970, as a nationwide street demonstration. Twenty million **Americans**[3] turned out to hear politicians speak about issues concerning the planet. People participated in everything from talkathons and prayer vigils to trail hikes. On Earth **Day**[4], **Girl**[5] Scout troops had children clean up the trash on the side of major highways. **Mrs**[6]. Sumi's group cleaned up **city**[7] parks and playgrounds. **The**[8] message was loud and clear. Every **American**[9] demanded action from their **state**[10] leaders because they were concerned about their environment. As a result, several environmental acts were passed in the 1970s. In 1970 alone, Congress responded by establishing the Environmental Protection Agency (**EPA**[11]) and passing the Clean Air Act. The Water Pollution Control Act, The Toxic Substance Control Act, and an **Endangered**[12] Species Act followed shortly after.

1. The – Capitalization: Capitalize the first word of a sentence.
2. April – Capitalization: Capitalize a month of the year.
3. Americans – Capitalization: Capitalize a nationality.
4. Day – Capitalization: Capitalize the name of a holiday.
5. Girl – Capitalization: Capitalize the name of a group.
6. Mrs. – Capitalization: Capitalize a person's title and its abbreviations.
7. city – Capitalization: Capitalize proper nouns only.
8. The – Capitalization: Capitalize the first word of a sentence.
9. Americans – Capitalization: Capitalize nationalities.
10. state – Capitalization: Do not capitalize federal or state if used as general terms.
11. EPA – Capitalization: Capitalize an acronym: **E**nvironmental **P**rotection **A**gency.
12. Endangered – Capitalization: Capitalize the first word of a title.

**7. Eclipsed!** (p. 10)

Stargazers from all over the **world**[1] converged near Hilo, **Hawaii**[2], during the new **moon**[3] to view a total solar eclipse. They came to spend a chilly morning in the **observatory**[4] atop the volcano **Mauna**[5] Kea, which is nearly 14,000 feet tall. As the moon hid more and more of the sun, the cheers began. **When**[6] the eclipse was total, the cheers became a deafening roar. It was a rare total eclipse visible from the Northern and **Western**[7] Hemispheres. Most eclipses can usually be seen only in the **Southern**[8] Hemisphere. The location was a real plus for **Gin**[9]-Wei Chang, a devoted observer. **"I've**[10] seen five in a row now, and this one is the best because I didn't have to travel so far," she said. "Last time, **I**[11] had to watch from an island in the Indian **Ocean**[12]." For all their preparation and excitement, the observers had little time to enjoy the view. The sun's total disappearance, which began at 11:07 a.m., lasted only four minutes.

1. world – Capitalization: Do not capitalize "world" because it is not a specific place.
2. Hawaii – Capitalization: Capitalize the names of states.
3. moon – Capitalization: Do not capitalize "moon" because it is not a star or planet.
4. observatory – Capitalization: Do not capitalize "observatory" because it is not a specific place.
5. Mauna – Capitalization: Capitalize the name of a place.
6. When – Capitalization: Capitalize the first word of a sentence.
7. Western – Capitalization: Capitalize compass points when they represent specific regions.
8. Southern – Capitalization: Capitalize compass points when they represent specific regions.
9. Gin – Capitalization: Capitalize a person's name.
10. I've – Capitalization: Capitalize the first word in a direct quotation.
11. I – Capitalization: Capitalize the pronoun I.
12. Ocean – Capitalization: Capitalize a geographical term following the name.

**8. Up in Arms** (p. 11)

31 **Post**[1] Road
**Cambridge**[2], MA 02138
**August**[3] 4, 2014

**Dear**[4] Kaneesha,

I was very happy to get the new job, but **I**[5] have felt like an octopus these last three weeks. It started out easy enough, but then **Ms**[6]. Atkins piled the work higher and higher. The sketch shows me dealing with the usual four phones at a time! I wouldn't mind so much if the **boss**[7] did some of the work herself. However, she often puts her feet up or even lies down for a nap like **Dad**[8] does! She says to me, **"Why**[9], you do almost as good a job as I do!" Isn't that awfully insulting? **Working**[10] here is neither fun nor profitable, and I couldn't care less for the job. It's time to look for a new one.

**Your**[11] **friend**[12],
Johann

1. Post – Capitalization: Capitalize the name of a road.
2. Cambridge – Capitalization: Capitalize the name of a city.
3. August – Capitalization: Capitalize a month of the year.
4. Dear – Capitalization: Capitalize the first word in the greeting in a letter.
5. I – Capitalization: Capitalize the pronoun I.
6. Ms. – Capitalization: Capitalize a person's title and its abbreviation.
7. boss – Capitalization: "Boss" is not a person's title, abbreviation, or nickname.
8. Dad – Capitalization: Capitalize a relationship when it substitutes for a person's name.
9. Why – Capitalization: Capitalize the first word in a direct quotation.
10. Working – Capitalization: Capitalize the first word of a sentence.
11. Your – Capitalization: Capitalize the first word in the closing in a letter.
12. friend – Capitalization: Capitalize only the first word in the closing in a letter.

**9. Drumming It In** (p. 17)

Most of my drumming moves were **okay,**[1] but I wanted to get even better. I was pretty excited when my instructor showed up at **4:30**[2]. **"Hey**[3], Professor, I'm so glad you came to **teach!**[4]" I said.

He got to the point. **"Let's**[5] see how you play now, and then we'll improve **it,"**[6] he replied. I played **"Tapper's Suite"**[7] better than ever, but my skills went unnoticed. **"First,**[8]" he began, "you must set the drum at elbow level. Then we'll work on your arms and hands." We positioned the drum, and I played again. "Your left **hand, which**[9] is weaker than your right, is lagging," he observed, "and, **what's**[10] worse, you're holding the stick **wrong."**[11] He made me hold my elbows **out,** grip the sticks **securely,**[12] and strike with the same force from each hand. I was happier before I knew how bad I **was.**[13]

1. okay, – Punctuation: Use a comma before a conjunction to join two simple sentences.
2. 4:30 – Punctuation: Use a colon to separate hours and minutes.
3. "Hey – Punctuation: Use quotation marks at the beginning of a direct quote.
4. teach! – Punctuation: Use an exclamation mark after a sentence that shows a strong emotion.
5. Let's – Punctuation: Use an apostrophe in contractions to show where letters (let us) have been left out.
6. it," – Punctuation: Use quotation marks at the end of a direct quotation.
7. "Tapper's Suite" – Punctuation: Use quotation marks to identify the title of a song.
8. "First," – Punctuation: Use a comma before and after the speaker in a divided quotation.
9. hand, which – Punctuation: Use a comma to set off sentence interrupters.
10. what's – Punctuation: Use an apostrophe in contractions to show where letters (what is) have been left out.
11. wrong." – Punctuation: Use quotation marks after ending punctuation.
12. out, securely, – Punctuation: Use a comma to separate words in a series.
13. was. – Punctuation: Use a period to end a declarative sentence.

**10. Letter to Madagascar** (p. 18)

University of Louisiana
Baton **Rouge,**[1] LA 70803
April **29,**[2] 2014

**Dr.**[3] Phillipe Tsirana
University of Madagascar
Antananarivo, Madagascar

Dear Dr. **Tsirana,**[4]

Thank you for assisting me in obtaining a travel visa. I will arrive at **4:00**[5] p.m. on June 6 and will stay for **twenty-six**[6] weeks to study the ring-tailed lemurs in their natural habitat. They live in the thorn forest and woodland in southwestern Madagascar. My article will be titled **"The**[7] Impact of Deforestation on Territorial Behavior in Ring-tailed **Lemurs."**[8] I plan to bring my daughter with me. She is 14 **(a young lady)**[9] and very excited about seeing Madagascar. I hope your **colleague, Yvette,**[10] will be in town when we arrive. We look forward to seeing you and her. **Oh,**[11] I almost forgot.

Who will be meeting us at the airport, and where should we **meet?**[12]

**Sincerely,**[13]
Dr. Neva Ledesma

1. Rouge, – Punctuation: Use a comma to separate a city and state.
2. 29, – Punctuation: Use a comma to separate the day of the month from the year.
3. Dr. – Punctuation: Use a period after an abbreviation.
4. Tsirana, – Punctuation: Use a comma in a friendly letter after the greeting.
5. 4:00 – Punctuation: Use a colon to separate hours and minutes.
6. twenty-six – Punctuation: Use a hyphen between compound numbers from twenty-one through ninety-nine.
7. "The – Punctuation: Use quotation marks to identify the title of an article.
8. Lemurs." – Punctuation: Use quotation marks after ending punctuation.
9. (a young lady) – Punctuation: Use parentheses to add information that is interesting but not very important.
10. colleague, Yvette, – Punctuation: Use commas to set off an appositive.
11. Oh, – Punctuation: Use a comma to separate an introductory word or interjection from the rest of the sentence.
12. meet? – Punctuation: Use a question mark after a question.
13. Sincerely, – Punctuation: Use a comma in a friendly letter following the closing.

**11. Mopping Up** (p. 19)

35 Lawsome **St.**[1]
**Jamesville,**[2] Iowa 95832
August **13,**[3] 2014

Dear Tonia,

Sam, my **roommate,**[4] has been taking the car to work. There are three **(3)**[5] things that I can **do:**[6] (a) I can take very short trips. (b) I can entertain myself at home. (c) I can ask a friend for a ride. I didn't want to take a … trip or ask … for a ride. I have found**, however,**[7] that lonely days are excellent for doing the housework. I said to myself, **"You**[8] should try it, **Tonia."**[9] This morning **three-fourths**[10] of my time has been dedicated to writing letters. As you can see from my enclosed sketch, I **haven't**[11] got much else to do until the kitchen floor **dries!**[12]

Your pal,
Jamal

1. St. – Punctuation: Use a period after an abbreviation.
2. Jamesville, – Punctuation: Use a comma to separate a city and state.
3. 13, – Punctuation: Use a comma to separate the day of the month from the year.
4. Sam, my roommate, – Punctuation: Use commas to set off an appositive.
5. (3) – Punctuation: Use parentheses to surround figures to make things clearer.
6. do: – Punctuation: Use a colon to precede a list when it follows a complete sentence.
7. , however, – Punctuation: Use a comma to separate an interjection from the rest of the sentence.
8. "You – Punctuation: Use quotation marks at the beginning of a direct quotation.
9. Tonia." – Punctuation: Use quotation marks after ending punctuation at the end of a direct quotation.
10. three-fourths – Punctuation: Use a hyphen in spelled-out fractions.
11. haven't – Punctuation: Use an apostrophe in contractions to show where letters (have not) have been left out.
12. dries! – Punctuation: Use an exclamation mark after a sentence that shows a strong emotion.

 

**12. Whale Watching Tours** (p. 20)

Three cruise lines offer expeditions to see **whales,**[1] but you should choose your sightseeing tour carefully. **"The**[2] pilots for Poseidon's Passages," Dad **explains,**[3] "run their boats the fastest of all. If the rolling of the waves makes you **sick,**[4] you could hardly experience a worse **ride."**[5] Many of my relatives agree. Some prefer the Atlantis Cruises. (Actually, I like **both.**[6]**)** Between you and me, I think **Frieda's**[7] Fleet, **(my favorite)**[8] offers a great tour. **You'll**[9] get a wonderful view of the whales as these acrobatic animals slice the water like **knives.**[10] Tours used to end at 6:00 **p.m.**[11], but now there are late boats running at **7:00**[12] for evening passengers. Would you like to go sometime **soon?**[13]

1. whales, – Punctuation: Use a comma before a conjunction to join two simple sentences.
2. "The – Punctuation: Use quotation marks at the beginning of a direct quotation.
3. explains, – Punctuation: Use a comma to separate the speaker from the quotation.
4. sick – Punctuation: Use a comma to set off an introductory phrase or dependent clause.
5. ride." – Punctuation: Use quotation marks after ending punctuation at the end of a direct quotation.
6. both.) – Punctuation: Periods go inside parentheses only if an entire sentence is inside the parentheses.
7. Frieda's – Punctuation: Use an apostrophe to form the possessive.
8. (my favorite) – Punctuation: Use parentheses to add information that is interesting, but not very important.
9. You'll – Punctuation: Use an apostrophe in contractions to show where letters (you will) have been left out.
10. knives. – Punctuation: Use a period to end a declarative sentence.
11. p.m. – Punctuation: Use a period after an abbreviation.
12. 7:00 – Punctuation: Use a colon to separate hours and minutes.
13. soon? – Punctuation: Use a question mark after a direct question.

**13. Pinto Show** (p. 21)

101 Pine St.
**Westville,**[1] NV 89500
July 8, 2014

Dear **Nina,**[2]

Please join me in Westville for the **annual**[3] pinto show! It will be better than ever because **Chairman**[4] Pavick has planned a lot of new activities. When you come, bring your partner so that you and he may compete in a mixed event. The Pinto Parade will be at **12:00**[5] on **Sunday**[6] at the corner of Main St. and King **St.**[7] An hour of various **women's**[8] and **men's**[9] competitions will follow. The show runs for only **five**[10] days, **Nina,**[11] so come as soon as you can. Be sure to mark those days in **July**[12] on your calendar **ASAP**[13] so you don't forget. **I**[14] look forward to seeing you there!

Your **friend**[15],
Sula

1. Westville, – Punctuation: Use a comma to separate a city and state.
2. Nina, – Punctuation: Use a comma in a friendly letter after the greeting.
3. annual – Content: See caption.
4. Chairman – Capitalization: Capitalize a person's title.
5. 12:00 – Punctuation: Use a colon to separate hours and minutes.
6. Sunday – Capitalization: Capitalize a day of the week.
7. King St. – Content: See picture.
8. women's – Punctuation: Add **'s** to form the possessive of plural nouns that do not end in s.
9. men's – Punctuation: Add **'s** to form the possessive of plural nouns that do not end in s.
10. five days – Content: See picture and caption (the 17th to the 21st is 5 days).
11. Nina, – Punctuation: Use a comma surrounding the name of a person directly addressed.
12. July – Content: See picture and caption.
13. ASAP – Capitalization: Capitalize an acronym: **A**s **S**oon **A**s **P**ossible.
14. I – Capitalization: Capitalize the pronoun I.

15. friend – Capitalization: Capitalize only the first word in the closing in a letter.

**14. The Missing Cookie Caper** (p. 22)

It was an ugly scene. **Chocolate**[1] fingerprints were smeared on the cookie jar, the kitchen **counter,**[2] and the younger **child's**[3] bedroom door. The culprit seemed obvious. **However,**[4] there were a few doubts. **Sean,**[5] the younger child, was five years old and only forty inches high. The **cookie**[6] jar was placed on a kitchen shelf about three feet above the counter. The counter was two feet from the ground. Suspicions began to turn to the older child, Jason. However, Jason was eight years old and only **four feet**[7] high. Furthermore, Jason's **right arm**[8] was in a cast. The **parents**[9] of the two boys were puzzled. **"Who**[10] could have done this?" **they**[11] asked. Both boys grinned from ear to ear as **Mom**[12] and **Dad**[13] scratched their heads!

1. Chocolate – Capitalization: Capitalize the first word of a sentence.
2. counter, – Punctuation: Use a comma to separate words in a series.
3. child's – Punctuation: Use an apostrophe to form the possessive.
4. However, – Punctuation: Use a comma to separate an introductory word from the rest of the sentence.
5. Sean, – Punctuation: Use a comma to set off a sentence interrupter.
6. cookie – Content: See caption.
7. four feet – Content: See caption.
8. right arm – Content: See picture.
9. parents – Punctuation: Do not use an apostrophe if a word is only plural.
10. "Who – Capitalization: Capitalize the first word of a quotation.
11. they – Capitalization: Capitalize only proper nouns.
12. Mom – Capitalization: Capitalize a relationship when it substitutes for a person's name.
13. Dad – Capitalization: Capitalize a relationship when it substitutes for a person's name.

**15. Fossil History** (p. 31)

Which came first on Earth? Was it the insects or the birds? A geologic timeline can tell us. **Geologists**[1] divide **Earth's**[2] history into various units of **time**[3], and the greatest unit of time is called an era. Our earliest fossil records of animal life on Earth date back to the **Paleozoic**[4] era. Insects appeared in the Paleozoic era and have remained unchanged for over 200 million years. The first birds, however, were **toothed**[5] and appeared in the **Mesozoic**[6] era during the Age of Reptiles. An age is a time period used by biologists to indicate when **one**[7] animal **species**[8] is **dominant**[9]. Modern **toothless**[10] birds did not develop until the **Cenozoic**[11] era. The earliest mammals appeared in the Mesozoic era, but the Age of Mammals did not begin until 130 million years later in the Cenozoic era.

1. Geologists – Spelling: Use the suffix -ist.
2. Earth's – Spelling: Add **'s** to form the singular possessive.
3. time – Spelling: (homophone) time is a particular period; thyme is a garden herb
4. Paleozoic – Spelling: The root word is paleo (G) – ancient, old.
5. toothed – Spelling: The digraph is spelled with a "th."
6. Mesozoic – Spelling: The root word is meso (G) – middle.
7. one – Spelling: (homophone) one is a single thing; won means finished first
8. species – Spelling: Some words don't change form at all for the singular and plural.
9. dominant – Spelling: Use the suffix -ant.
10. toothless – Spelling: Use the suffix -less.
11. Cenozoic – Spelling: The root word is zo (G) – animal.

**16. The Wright Stuff** (p. 32)

Many people know that on December 17, 1903, Orville and Wilbur Wright brought powered flight to humans. Other events in the **Wrights'**[1] lives may not be as well known. In the early years, the two sold **bicycles**[2]. They could **have**[3] continued in the bicycle business, but they developed an interest in **aeronautics**[4]. They experimented with gliders and built a wind **tunnel**[5] to test various wing shapes. For less than $1,000, the **two**[6] men eventually designed and built the first power airplane. Wilbur was the first to attempt to fly it because he had won a coin toss for the honor. **It's**[7] hard to believe that **their**[8] hometown newspaper did **not**[9] even cover this momentous event. In 1903, who would **have**[10] guessed that the skies **would**[11] soon be **ours**[12]?

1. Wrights' – Spelling: Add an apostrophe to form the possessive of a plural word ending in -s.
2. bicycles – Spelling: The root word is cycl (G) – circle.
3. have – Spelling: "Of " should not be used for "have."
4. aeronautics – Spelling: The word roots are aero (G) – air and naut (G) – sailor, ship.
5. tunnel – Spelling: Often the consonant is doubled in the middle of words that have two syllables and short vowel sounds in both syllables.
6. two – Spelling: (homophone) <u>two</u> means the name of the numeral "2"; <u>too</u> means also
7. It's – Spelling: (homophone) <u>it's</u> is the contraction for "it is"; <u>its</u> is the possessive form of "it"
8. their – Spelling: (homophone) <u>their</u> means "belonging to them"; <u>they're</u> is the contraction for "they are"
9. not – Spelling: (homophone) <u>not</u> is used to show denial; <u>knot</u> means a knob to connect two cords together
10. have – Spelling: "Of" should not be used for "have."
11. would – Spelling: Do not use the digraph "wh" in the spelling of "would."
12. ours – Spelling: A possessive pronoun does not use an apostrophe to form the possessive.

**17. A Note on the Trumpet** (p. 33)

Hey, I'm **no**[1] slacker! I did some research when I started playing the trumpet. The **early**[2] trumpet dates back to 2000 B.C. That first trumpet was a lot different from mine. It was probably made from a shell. It had no valves, but players lent different qualities to their tones by altering the **shapes**[3] of their mouths. With **today's**[4] trumpet, **you**[5] can still play a **lot**[6] of tones without pressing any of the valves. I myself have played a simple song this way. With three valves, though, I can play all of the notes in my range. I play an A **using**[7] my first **two**[8] valves, and I press just the first **valve**[9] to play an F. With all the **possible**[10] **combinations**[11], I'll bet I can play better than those early trumpeters!

1. no – Spelling: (homophone) <u>no</u> is used to express denial; <u>know</u> means to understand
2. early – Spelling: Use **y** to make the long /e/ sound at the end of words.
3. shapes – Spelling: Use the consonant digraph "sh" to represent the consonant sound /sh/.
4. today's trumpet – Spelling: Use **'s** to form the singular possessive.
5. you – Spelling: (homophone) <u>you</u> refers to people in general; <u>ewe</u> is a female sheep
6. a lot – Spelling: A lot is two words.
7. using – Spelling: Drop the silent "e" from a word when adding a vowel suffix.
8. two – Spelling: (homophone) <u>two</u> is the name of the numeral "2"; <u>to</u> means "in a direction toward"
9. valve – Spelling: A silent "e" needs to be added at the end of the word.
10. possible – Spelling: Use the suffix -ible.
11. combinations – Spelling: Use the prefix com-.

**18. Flying Mammals** (p. 34)

Bats are the only mammals that can truly fly. Flying squirrels and flying lemurs actually glide. **Bats'**[1] wings are formed by a membrane that stretches between the bones of their hands. The structure of birds' wings is different. A **bird's**[2] wings are formed from the arm bones. Bats are **nocturnal**[3], yet most have poor eyesight. These bats with poor eyesight use **echolocation**[4] to guide **their**[5] flights. They make **supersonic**[6] sounds in their throats. They use the echoes from these sounds to guide **themselves**[7] and find food. Most echolocating bats **actually**[8] catch small insects **while**[9] flying in the air. In 1940, a **chiropterologist**[10] by the name of Donald Griffin, **revolutionized**[11] bat research when he discovered bats' use of echolocation. Few scientists have done more to fascinate the public about bats.

1. Bats' – Spelling: Add an apostrophe to form the possessive of a plural word ending in -s.
2. bird's – Spelling: Add **'s** to form the singular possessive.
3. nocturnal – Spelling: The root word is noct (L) – night.
4. echolocation – Spelling: The root word is echo (G) – sound.
5. their – Spelling: (homophone) their means "belonging to them"; there refers to a place
6. supersonic – Spelling: The root is son (L) – sound.
7. themselves – Spelling: The plural of themself is formed by changing the "f" to "v" and adding -es.
8. actually – Spelling: Use the suffix -ly.
9. while – Spelling: Use the consonant digraph "wh" to correctly spell the word "while."
10. chiropterologist – Spelling: The root words are chiro (G) – hand and ptero (G) – wing, feather.
11. revolutionized – Spelling: Drop a silent "e" from a word when adding a vowel suffix.

**19.** (p. 35)

1. b. The beauty queen was asked to lead the parade on a spectacular float.
2. a. Some music is written specifically for bass singers.
3. b. Phones used to have only one kind of ring.
4. b. We each had a big bowl of popcorn.
5. a. When you pet his back, he will purr.
6. c. Did Taylor use a pen or a pencil?
7. c. The dove was as white as snow.
8. a. His employer had to fire him for continual tardiness.

**20.** Answers will vary. (p. 36)
Examples below:

2. a. When he stopped coming in for work, his boss gave him the boot.
   b. While walking through the pasture, she got manure on her boot.
3. a. Her New Year's Resolution was to get into shape.
   b. The potter will shape his new project into a sphere.
4. a. "It is not polite to point," the mother reminded her son.
   b. The point of my pencil has become dull.
5. a. I look forward to the blossoms in spring!
   b. My mattress spring is poking me.
   c. We watched the panther spring into action.
6. a. The new mother reluctantly dropped her baby off at the nursery.
   b. This weekend we will go to the nursery and select new plants for our garden.
7. a. Nobody won because it was a tie!
   b. When my dad has an important meeting, he wears his red tie.
   c. Eric is just learning to tie his shoes.
8. a. The toddlers were learning to share their toys.
   b. I want my share of the winnings!
9. a. My parents put a fence around the front yard.
   b. Thirty six inches equals a yard.
10. a. When my brother eats quickly, my parents tell him not to shovel his food.
    b. This new shovel will help me in my yard.
11. a. Did you pack your warm jacket?
    b. Ashley has a new pack for hiking.

**21. A Net Gain** (p. 42)

In **a**[1] stunning upset in the National Junior Tennis Championships, Marie O'Neal defeated **heavily**[2] favored Alicia Alfonso. O'Neal upset **two**[3] other favored players on the way to her first national crown. In the title match, she lost her serve only in **the**[4] last game of the second set. Alfonso's serve, in contrast, was broken **once**[5] in the first set and once in the third set. She had not lost her serve in the **previous**[6] three matches. O'Neal was happy that her hard work paid off. "This makes me very **proud**[7]," she said, "and I hope to do as well next year."

Alfonso thought her opponent deserved to win and said, "Marie played very well **today**[8]. She kept **the**[9] ball deep and won the big points. She has a **tough**[10] right-handed serve."

O'Neal planned to take some time off to enjoy her big win. Alfonso planned to return to her Cincinnati home to continue training. **Both**[11] players will try to qualify for the U.S. Open **later**[12] this year.

1. a – Article: Use **a** before a word that begins with a consonant sound.
2. heavily – Adverb: Use an adverb to describe to what extent something happens.
3. two – Adjective: Use an adjective to describe how many players.
4. the – Article: Use **the** when referring to something in particular (game).
5. once – Adverb: Use an adverb to describe how often something happens.
6. previous – Adjective: Use an adjective to describe which match.
7. proud – Adjective: Use an adjective to describe the pronoun me.
8. today – Adverb: Use an adverb to describe when something happens.
9. the – Article: Use **the** when referring to something in particular (ball).
10. tough – Adjective: Use an adjective to describe what kind of serve.
11. Both – Adjective: Use an adjective to tell how many players.
12. later – Adverb: Use an adverb to describe when something happens.

**22. A.S.A.P. for the S.P.C.A.!** (p. 43)

What are you doing this summer? Does the thought of rescuing wild animals, caring for stray cats and dogs, or helping out with a **charitable**[1] event sound fun? If you are **an**[2] animal lover and would like to get involved in one of the best charitable organizations in town, then join the Society for **the**[3] Prevention of Cruelty to Animals. **Today**[4] with **more**[5] than 200 animals living at our facility, we are **always**[6] in need of good volunteers. Handling dogs and cats, caring for wildlife, and working with the public are the **greatest**[7] opportunities **available**[8] to all of our new volunteers. After you see **these**[9] animals, you will want to become their friend. In return, they will **eagerly**[10] be good friends to you. Our next volunteer orientation is Monday, June 2 at 2:00 p.m. **inside**[11] our administration building. Playful paws and **a**[12] good time await your arrival!

1. charitable – Adjective: Use an adjective to describe what kind of event.
2. an – Article: Use **an** before a word that begins with a vowel sound.
3. the – Article: Use **the** when referring to something in particular.
4. Today – Adverb: Use an adverb to describe when something happens.
5. more – Adjective: Use a comparative irregular adjective to compare two things.
6. always – Adverb: Use an adverb to describe when something happens.
7. greatest – Adjective: Use a superlative adjective to compare three or more things (opportunities).
8. available – Adjective: Use an adjective to describe what kind of opportunity.
9. these – Adjective: Use an adjective to describe which animals.
10. eagerly – Adverb: Use an adverb to describe how something happens.
11. inside – Adverb: Use an adverb to describe where something happens.
12. a – Article: Use **a** before a word that begins with a consonant sound.

**23. Deadly Dino** (p. 44)

Tyrannosaurus rex was the **most**[1] feared predator of its time. It could run very fast on its **powerful**[2] hind legs, and its sharp teeth were **effective**[3] in catching its food. Tyrannosaurus rex and other dinosaurs first appeared about 200 million years ago. They became extinct **approximately**[4] 65 million years ago. For **more**[5] than 135 million years, dinosaurs ruled the world. Tyrannosaurus rex was **the**[6] king of them all. The T-rex, as it is **popularly**[7] called, had two long hind legs that it used for walking or running and two **shorter**[8] front legs that it used for attacking its prey. Even at 20 feet tall, the T-rex was not the **tallest**[9] of all dinosaurs. That was **an**[10] honor belonging to brachiosaurus, which could have looked over a building three stories high. The ability to catch and eat other dinosaurs made T-rex an **intensely**[11] feared predator of prehistoric times.

1. most – Adjective: Use a superlative irregular adjective to compare three or more things.

2. powerful – Adjective: Use an adjective to describe what kind of legs.
3. effective – Adjective: Use an adjective to describe what kind of teeth.
4. approximately – Adverb: Use an adverb to describe when something happens.
5. more – Adjective: Use a comparative irregular adjective to describe a greater amount.
6. the – Article: Use **the** when referring to something in particular.
7. popularly – Adverb: Use an adverb to describe how something happens.
8. shorter – Adjective: Use a comparative adjective to compare two things.
9. tallest – Adjective: Use a superlative adjective to compare three or more things.
10. an – Article: Use **an** before a word that begins with a vowel sound.
11. intensely – Adverb: Use an adverb to describe to what extent something happens.

**24. Wish You Were Here** (p. 45)

The Polynesian Islands have been a **healthy**[1] change for Tia and me. We have a great view of **the**[2] ocean and the palm trees from our **thatched**[3] hut. Our favorite food here is the coconut, the sweet fruit of **a**[4] tree called the coconut palm.

**Yesterday**[5], Auntie called from home and said, "Bring me back **some**[6] fresh coconuts. Our **best**[7] ones are not even as good as your **worst**[8] ones. Get them to Riley and me this spring." I'm afraid my aunt and uncle will **certainly**[9] have to wait until after spring. Even by June, Tia and I will not have spent **enough**[10] time **here**[11]!

1. healthy – Adjective: Use an adjective to describe what kind of change.
2. the – Article: Use **the** when referring to something in particular.
3. thatched – Adjective: Use an adjective to describe what kind of hut.
4. a – Article: Use **a** before a word that begins with a consonant sound.
5. Yesterday – Adverb: Use an adverb to describe when something happens.
6. some – Adjective: Use an adjective to describe how many.
7. best – Adjective: Use a superlative irregular adjective to compare three or more things.
8. worst – Adjective: Use a superlative irregular adjective to compare three or more things.
9. certainly – Adverb: Use an adverb to describe to what extent something happens.
10. enough – Adverb: Use an adverb to describe to what extent something happens.
11. here – Adverb: Use an adverb to describe where something happens.

**25. A Profitable Platform** (p. 50)

Dear Editor:

As part **of**[1] my campaign platform for student body president, I would like to propose **that**[2] students be paid for attending school. My mom is always telling me that school is my job. Students would learn much faster than usual if they got paid for it, **and**[3] they would obtain valuable experience in earning a living. **If**[4] I had been paid $5.00 for each hour I attended school last semester, I would have earned a whole lot more **than**[5] I did. When my parents paid me **for**[6] the two A's that I earned on my report **card,**[7] I got only received $10. **Why**[8] should my grades improve? The school could establish **both**[9] a salary scale based on letter grades **and**[10] pay each of us students an hourly wage based **on**[11] our previous semester's academic performance. I know mine would surely improve. **After**[12] the school administration gives my request due consideration, I hope that the students will be able to vote on this important issue **so**[13] things can change.

Sincerely,
Justin Case

1. of – Preposition: Use **of** so the sentence makes sense.
2. that – Conjunction: Use a subordinating conjunction to introduce an independent clause.
3. and – Conjunction: Use a coordinating conjunction to join two simple sentences.
4. If – Conjunction: Use a subordinating conjunction to introduce an independent clause.
5. than – Conjunction: Use a subordinating conjunction to introduce an independent clause.

6. for – Preposition: Use **for** so the sentence makes sense.
7. card, – Conjunction: When a sentence consists of a dependent clause followed by an independent clause, the dependent clause should be followed by a comma.
8. Why – Conjunction: Use a subordinating conjunction to introduce an independent clause.

9/10. both/and – Conjunction: Use correlative conjunctions to join similar ideas in a sentence.

11. on – Preposition: Use **on** so the sentence makes sense.
12. After – Preposition: Use **after** so the sentence makes sense.
13. so – Conjunction: Use a coordinating conjunction to join two simple sentences.

**26. Making Maple Syrup** (p. 51)

Large sugar bush operators now have pipeline systems, **but**[1] small farmers still gather sap **from**[2] sugar maple trees by hand as if that is easy! They empty the sap into a big tub **and**[3] drive it **by tractor and wagon**[4] to the sugar shanty where the liquid is boiled. It takes **about**[5] forty gallons of sap to make one gallon of syrup.

Since this has been a tough year, Claire and Dave Bevy are looking for help. "You can watch and learn **from**[6] us experts," they say, "so you will do well. **Either**[7] you can watch and learn, **or**[8] there are times you can help out. Then if you ask permission to taste the sweet and sticky **samples,**[9] our answer will be that you may. **After**[10] a day of making maple syrup, you will be very tired **because**[11] you will have had a lot of fun!"

1. but – Conjunction: Use a coordinating conjunction to join two simple sentences.
2. from – Preposition: Use **from** so the sentence makes sense.
3. and – Conjunction: Use a coordinating conjunction to join a clause and a phrase.
4. by tractor and by wagon – Preposition: When two words or phrases require the same preposition, do not use the preposition twice.
5. about – Preposition: Use **about** so the sentence makes sense.
6. from – Preposition: Use **from** so the sentence makes sense.

7/8. Either/or – Conjunction: Use correlative conjunctions to join similar ideas in a sentence.

9. samples, – Conjunction: When a sentence consists of a dependent clause followed by an independent clause, the dependent clause should be followed by a comma.
10. After – Conjunction: Use a subordinating conjunction to introduce an independent clause.
11. because – Conjunction: Use a subordinating conjunction to introduce an independent clause.

**27. Rash Results** (p. 52)

In the Western woods, don't be rash **where**[1] you hike. You must watch out for poison oak, **because**[2] Madeleine Vu found this **out**[3] the hard way while walking in California. "Poison oak is closely related to poison ivy,[4] and it also has leaves made up **of**[5] three leaflets. The plant contains oil that causes a skin reaction **when**[6] you touch it. I could get poison oak not **only**[7] through direct contact with the plant, **but**[8] also through contact with anything the plant has touched. I could get it **from**[9] my dog or even my clothing. **How**[10] would you like to be covered **with**[11] itchy red spots like mine?" Madeleine asks. "You may be sorry, **so**[12] watch what's around you. Your rash will remind you for a very long time **that**[13] you still need to be careful."

1. where – Conjunction: Use a subordinating conjunction to introduce an independent clause.
2. because – Conjunction: Use a subordinating conjunction to introduce an independent clause.
3. out – Preposition: Use **out** so the sentence makes sense.
4. ivy, – Conjunction: When a coordinating conjunction joins two independent clauses, or main clauses, it should be preceded by a comma unless the independent clauses are short and closely related.

5. of – Preposition: Use **of** so the sentence makes sense.
6. when – Conjunction: Use a subordinating conjunction to introduce an independent clause.

7/8. not only/but also – Conjunction: Use correlative conjunctions to join similar ideas in a sentence.

9. from – Preposition: Use **from** so the sentence makes sense.
10. how – Conjunction: Use a subordinating conjunction to introduce an independent clause.
11. With – Preposition: Use **with** so the sentence makes sense.
12. so – Conjunction: Use a coordinating conjunction to join a clause and a phrase.
13. that – Conjunction: Use a subordinating conjunction to separate the independent clause and the dependent clause.

**28. Rescue** (p. 53)

One spring day, Jorge and his friend Antonio went hiking on Mt. Mateo **while**[1] it was raining. Jorge decided to take a route that looked shorter than the normal trail **even though**[2] it didn't look very safe. The slope he was climbing suddenly gave way **so that**[3] Jorge was caught **in**[4] a rock slide. He slid 60 feet, fell **from**[5] a cliff that was 15 feet high, and came to rest **on**[6] an inaccessible plateau. He had broken his leg and bruised his ribs, **because**[7] he had fallen. Jorge was unable to climb the rocky slope, **so**[8] he waited while Antonio went for help. Jorge was relieved **when**[9] he looked **to**[10] the west and saw the helicopter dropping him a lifeline. "**Although**[11] it was quite an ordeal," Jorge said of the men's experience, "he and I have learned to stick closer to the trail, **provided**[12] we go again."

1. while – Conjunction: Use a subordinating conjunction to introduce a dependent clause.
2. even though – Conjunction: Use a subordinating conjunction to introduce an independent clause.
3. so that – Conjunction: Use a subordinating conjunction to introduce an independent clause.
4. in – Preposition: Use **in** so the sentence makes sense.
5. from – Preposition: Use **from** so the sentence makes sense.
6. on – Preposition: Use **on** so the sentence makes sense.
7. because – Conjunction: Use a subordinating conjunction to introduce an independent clause.
8. so – Conjunction: Use a coordinating conjunction to join two simple sentences.
9. when – Conjunction: Use a subordinating conjunction to introduce an independent clause.
10. to – Preposition: Use **to** so the sentence makes sense.
11. Although –Conjunction: Use a subordinating conjunction to introduce an independent clause.
12. provided – Conjunction: Use a subordinating conjunction to introduce an independent clause.

**29. A Pirate's Life for Me?** (p. 54)

"Yo ho, yo ho, **it's**[1] a pirate's life for me!" Why **not**[2]? A pirate's life was filled with adventure, danger, and much excitement! Well, that wasn't **really**[3] the case. Pirates' lives were not as glamorous as books have portrayed them. Pirates made **their**[4] living attacking merchant ships and coastal towns. The **battles**[5] were **brutal,**[6] and a pirate rarely lived **long**[7]. Pirates were considered outlaws **by**[8] all nations. They sailed under their own flag, the skull and **crossbones, and**[9] they lived by their own loose system of rules. These rules specified the share of the treasure each pirate **received**[10] and the amount of **compensation**[11] for lost limbs and other injuries. However, very few of the pirates actually shared in the lavish treasure **chests of jewels and gold**[12]. **Most**[13] were very **poor, and**[14] many fared **worse**[15] than beggars.

1. it's – Spelling: (homophone) it's is the contraction for "it is"; its is the possessive form of "it"
2. not – Spelling: (homophone) not is used to show denial; knot means a knob to connect two cords together
3. really – Adverb: Use an adverb to emphasize the verb.

4. their – Spelling: (homophone) their means "belonging to them"; they're is the contraction for "they are"
5. battles – Spelling: Double the consonant in the middle of words that have two syllables and short vowel sounds in both syllables.
6. brutal, – Conjunction: When a coordinating conjunction joins two independent clauses, or main clauses, it should be preceded by comma unless the independent clauses are short and closely related.
7. long – Adjective: Use an adjective to describe the length of a pirate's life.
8. by – Preposition: Use **by** so the sentence makes sense.
9. crossbones, and – Conjunction: When a coordinating conjunction joins two independent clauses, or main clauses, it should be preceded by comma unless the independent clauses are short and closely related.
10. received – Conjunction: When a dependent clause begins with a subordinating conjunction and follows an independent clause, no comma is required.
11. compensation – Spelling: The root word is pens (L) – hang, weigh.
12. chests of jewels and gold – Preposition: When two words or phrases require the same preposition, do not use the preposition twice.
13. Most – Adjective: Use a superlative irregular adjective to compare three or more things.
14. poor, and – Conjunction: When a coordinating conjunction joins two independent clauses, or main clauses, it should be preceded by comma unless the independent clauses are short and closely related.
15. worse – Adjective: Use a comparative irregular adjective to compare two things.

**30. Do Elephants Mourn?** (p. 55)

Do elephants mourn the loss of other elephants? **A lot**[1] of scientists have wondered about this. It's a question that has no **definite**[2] **answer, but**[3] fascinating behaviors have been observed. There are documented cases of elephants gathering around the body of a deceased **elephant**[4] and staying with it for as long as a **week**[5] to protect it from scavengers. Seeing the remains of **a**[6] tusk has prompted some elephants to stop, pick the tusk up with their trunks, caress **it,**[7] and then pass it among **themselves**[8]. Some **elephants**[9] have been observed trying to pick up a fallen and wounded elephant with their trunks in an attempt to help the fallen elephant to its feet again. Perhaps we will never **know**[10] if elephants **mourn, but**[11] it is a **good**[12] question to ponder. What do **you**[13] think?

1. A lot – Spelling: A lot is two words.
2. definite – Adjective: Use an adjective to describe what kind of answer.
3. answer, but – Conjunction: When a coordinating conjunction joins two independent clauses, or main clauses, it should be preceded by comma unless the independent clauses are short and closely related.
4. elephant – Conjunction: When a dependent clause beginning with a subordinating conjunction follows an independent clause, no comma is required.
5. week – Spelling: (homophone) week means 7 days; weak means not strong
6. a – Article: Use **a** before a word that begins with a consonant sound.
7. it, – Coordinating conjunction: When a coordinating conjunction joins two independent clauses, or main clauses, it should be preceded by a comma unless the independent clauses are short and closely related.
8. themselves – Spelling: The plural of themself is formed by changing the "f" to "v" and adding -es.
9. elephants – Spelling: Do not use an apostrophe if a word is only plural.
10. know – Spelling: (homophone) know means to understand; no is used to express denial
11. mourn, but – Conjunction: When a coordinating conjunction joins two independent clauses, or main clauses, it should be preceded by comma unless the independent clauses are short and closely related.

12. good – Adjective: Use an adjective to describe what kind of question.
13. you – Spelling: (homophone) you refers to people; ewe means a female sheep

**31. The Planetarium** (p. 56)

Next week our class is going **on**[1] a trip to the planetarium. We'll be leaving at **8:30**[2] on **Fri.**[3] morning. I've only been there once before, so needless to say, I'm **really**[4] looking forward to going back there. You can expect light-years of travel during **your**[5] visit to a planetarium. Special lights that are **shone**[6] on the **curved**[7] ceiling of the planetarium simulate the movements of the **stars**[8]. Music and narration help set the mood. You can enjoy a view **of**[9] the present night **sky,**[10] or you can see how **the**[11] stars will appear in the future. On my first planetarium trip, **I**[12] saw the summer sky and many other scenes. My favorite scene was this view from the **moon's**[13] surface. I felt as though I was sitting on the **moon's**[14] cratered surface.

1. on – Preposition: Use **on** so the sentence makes sense.
2. 8:30 – Punctuation: Use a colon to separate hours and minutes.
3. Fri. – Punctuation: Use a period at the end of an abbreviation.
4. really – Adverb: Use an adverb to emphasize the verb.
5. your – Spelling: (homophone) your means belonging to you; you're is the contraction for "you are"
6. shone – Spelling: When the letter "e" is at the end of a word, it's usually silent.
7. curved – Content: See picture and caption.
8. stars – Capitalization: Capitalize only proper nouns.
9. of – Preposition: Use **of** so the sentence makes sense.
10. sky, or – Conjunction: When a coordinating conjunction joins two independent clauses, or main clauses, it should be preceded by comma unless the independent clauses are short and closely related.
11. the – Article: Use **the** when referring to something in particular.
12. I – Capitalization: Capitalize the pronoun I.
13. moon's – Content: See picture and caption. (Earth appears in the background, so you cannot be viewing from Earth; also, the caption states the spectators feel as if they are sitting on the moon's cratered surface.) (Acceptable: view of Earth's surface OR view of Earth)
14. moon's – Capitalization: Capitalize only proper nouns.

**32. Plane Scary** (p. 57)

The Barnstormers Air Show at Blue Skies Airport was **heavily**[1] clouded with smoke on **Sunday**[2] after Jan Fay's **biplane**[3] burst into flames. As Fay fell toward the **ground,**[4] a fully opened parachute appeared over her head.

"The **Federal**[5] Aviation Administration and the airport manager are reviewing the case," said **Investigator**[6] Lin. "The fact that we **can't**[7] prevent air **show**[8] disasters is **most**[9] **unfortunate."**[10]

Jan Fay has flown for years, **but**[11] piloting **no**[12] longer interests her as much as constructing model airplanes. Next **June,**[13] she will begin her new hobby in earnest.

1. heavily – Adverb: Use an adverb to describe to what extent something happens.
2. Sunday – Content: See picture and caption.
3. biplane – Content: See picture and caption.
4. ground, – Punctuation: Use a comma to set off an introductory phrase or dependent clause.
5. Federal – Capitalization: Capitalize federal or state when used as part of an official agency name where these terms represent an official name.
6. Investigator – Capitalization: Capitalize a person's title.
7. can't – Punctuation: Use an apostrophe in contractions (cannot) to show where letters have been left out.
8. show – Spelling: The consonant digraph "sh" represents the consonant sound /sh/.
9. most – Adjective: Use a superlative irregular adjective to compare three or more things.
10. unfortunate." – Punctuation: Use quotation marks at the end of a direct quote.
11. but – Conjunction: Use a coordinating

 

conjunction to join two simple sentences.

12. no – Spelling: (homophone) no is used to express denial; know means to understand
13. June, – Punctuation: Use a comma to set off an introductory phrase or dependent clause.

**33. Fishy Story** (p. 58)

I had been diving in the **South**[1] Pacific and studying the local sea life. I'm afraid I came a bit closer to a certain form of sea life than I truly desired. **Let's**[2] call her Wanda. Though I moved the **fastest**[3] I have ever moved, I could not escape her gaping jaws. **Thirty-four**[4] teeth surrounded **me,**[5] and they threatened to clamp down harder at any moment. My **scuba**[6] gear seemed to be squeezing my head **more**[7] tightly than ever. My arms were just about to give out. **Fortunately,**[8] **Captain**[9] **Drake**[10] appeared and came **quickly**[11] to my rescue. He was able to prop **Wanda's**[12] mouth open with a long beam while I escaped. Wanda is **probably**[13] now telling her friends about the **one**[14] that got away!

1. South – Capitalization: Capitalize compass points when they represent specific regions.
2. Let's – Punctuation: Use an apostrophe in contractions to show where letters (let us) have been left out.
3. fastest – Adjective: Use a superlative adjective to compare three or more things.
4. Thirty-four – Punctuation: Use a hyphen between compound numbers from twenty-one through ninety-nine.
5. me, and – Conjunction: When a coordinating conjunction joins two independent clauses, or main clauses, it should be preceded by a comma unless the independent clauses are short and closely related.
6. scuba – Content: See picture.
7. more – Adverb: Use an adverb to describe to what extent something happens.
8. Fortunately, – Punctuation: Use a comma to separate an introductory word or interjection from the rest of the sentence.
9. Captain – Capitalization: Capitalize a person's title.
10. Drake – Content: See caption.
11. quickly – Adverb: Use an adverb to describe how something happens.
12. Wanda's – Spelling: Add **'s** to form the possessive of plural nouns that do not end in s.
13. probably – Spelling: To make the long "e" sound at the end of a word use **y**.
14. one – Spelling: (homophone) one is a single thing; won means finished first

**34. A Lesson on Haiku** (p. 59)

"Is this a haiku **poem?"**[1] Mr. Zaluski asked the class. The **students'**[2] eyes scanned the poem in **their**[3] literature books. **"How**[4] is a haiku poem arranged?" the teacher questioned.

"**A**[5] haiku poem has seventeen syllables. It's arranged in three lines of five, **seven**[6], and five syllables **each,"**[7] Roberto replied.

"**Excellent,**[8] Roberto. You have been doing your homework. The haiku is a traditional form of **Japanese**[9] poetry that was developed in the **1600s**[10] by a man named Basho. What do you notice about haiku?" Mr. Zaluski asked.

"It's simple," Shakira stated.

"Yes, the haiku seems simple because there are few words," Mr. Zaluski replied. However, it is meant to express something much more."

Carmen rose to the **challenge**[11]. "Maybe the poet is trying to express **serenity, or**[12] on the other hand, maybe the flower is meant to symbolize renewal of life,"

Mr. Zaluski smiled. His class was **really**[13] catching on.

1. poem?" – Punctuation: Use quotation marks after ending punctuation.
2. students' – Spelling: Add an apostrophe to form the possessive of a plural word ending in **-s**, **-es**, or **-ies**.
3. their – Spelling: (homophone) their means "belonging to them"; there refers to a place
4. "How – Capitalization: Capitalize the first word in a quotation.
5. A – Article: Use **a** before a word that begins with a consonant sound.
6. seven – Content: See picture.
7. each," – Punctuation: Use a comma to separate the speaker from the quotation.
8. Excellent, Roberto – Punctuation: Use a comma surrounding the name of a person directly addressed.
9. Japanese – Capitalization: Capitalize a

nationality.
10. 1600s – Content: See caption.
11. challenge – Spelling: Double the consonant in the middle of a word that has two syllables and short vowel sounds in both syllables.
12. serenity, or – Conjunction: When a coordinating conjunction joins two independent clauses, or main clauses, it should be preceded by a comma unless the independent clauses are short and closely related.
13. really – Adverb: Adverbs describe verbs.

**35. A Glimpse Into the Past** (p. 66)

Tucson, Arizona
January 29, 2011

Dear Linda,

I haven't written since **my**[1] letter of December 22, 2010, because I've been busy writing a report about Machu Picchu. This hidden city is 8,000 feet high and was built by the Incas in South America. The Incas were conquered in the 1500s, but **many**[2] of **them**[3] fled to this secret city. **It**[4] remained undiscovered for about another 400 years. I read and am sending you "Secrets of the Past," an article that gives **us**[5] many facts about the ruins. It shows a stone wall with a man **who**[6] is only a third as tall. I also read, "Inca Treasures," a popular story about an Inca man. **Some**[7] liked the story but **they**[8] learned more from the article. **Both**[9] gave me a glimpse to the world of the Incas. **Their**[10] lives were far different from **ours**[11] in Tucson, Arizona, today!

Your friend,
Azzi

1. my – Pronoun: Use the correct form of the possessive pronoun before a noun.
2. many – Pronoun: An indefinite pronoun is used to indicate quantity.
3. them – Pronoun: "Them" is an objective pronoun; "they" is a subjective pronoun.
4. It – Pronoun: "It" is referring to the city Machu Picchu, not a person.
5. us – Pronoun: "Us" is an objective pronoun; "we" is a subjective pronoun.
6. who – Pronoun: "Who" functions as a subject.
7. Some – Pronoun: An indefinite pronoun does not refer to a specific person or thing. Indefinite pronouns are often used to make general statements or to indicate quantity.
8. they – Pronoun: "They" is a subjective pronoun; "them" is an objective pronoun.
9. Both – Pronoun: "Both" is referring to the two articles.
10. Their – Pronoun: Use a possessive pronoun to show ownership.
11. ours – Pronoun: Use a possessive pronoun to show ownership.

**36. An Early American** (p. 67)

**We**[1] could hardly wait to hear the author of "Early American Animals"! "Had you lived during the 1830s, **you**[2] might have seen great herds of bison grazing between the Appalachian Mountains and the Rockies," he began. "Though **many**[3] of these majestic creatures were wiped out, **some**[4] are still around today."

We interrupted **him**[5]. "How would you know a pair of bison if they **themselves**[6] walked down your street?" we asked.

"Well," he answered, "**most**[7] bison's hair is coarse and brown. **These**[8] have a hump on their back. Two horns adorn each massive head, and the bison wear beards under **their**[9] chins. A bull weighs close to a ton, but a cow weighs half as much. When provoked, **each**[10] of the two bison could probably run quite fast. Let's hope **you**[11] would run the fastest!"

We were glad that **our**[12] hero had both knowledge and a sense of humor.

1. We – Pronoun: "We" is a subjective pronoun; "us" is an objective pronoun.
2. you – Pronoun: Use a personal pronoun to replace one or more nouns. OR "You" is a subjective pronoun; "yours" is a possessive pronoun.
3. many – Pronoun: Use an indefinite pronoun to indicate quantity.
4. some – Pronoun: Use an indefinite pronoun to indicate to quantity.
5. him – Pronoun: Use a personal pronoun to replace one or more nouns. OR "Him" is an objective pronoun; "his" is a possessive pronoun.
6. themselves – Pronoun: Use the plural form

of the reflexive pronoun.

7. most – Pronoun: Use an indefinite pronoun indicate quantity.
8. These – Pronoun: "These" is nearby; "those" is farther away.
9. their – Pronoun: Possessive pronouns show ownership and don't need an s. OR "Their" is a possessive pronoun; "theirs" is a subjective pronoun.
10. each – Pronoun: Use an indefinite pronoun to indicate quantity.
11. you – Pronoun: Use a subjective personal pronoun.
12. our – Pronoun: Possessive pronouns show ownership and don't need an s. OR "Our" is a possessive pronoun; "ours" is a subjective pronoun.

**37. Animated About Art** (p. 68)

**We**[1] were excited to hear about jobs at Magic Carpet Studios! We readily lent **our**[2] ears to Supervisor Warren of the animation team. "Layout artists make sketches of **all**[3] scenes for the animated film. Background artists create tone and style, and each animator designs a character. Have **you**[4] any idea how much research is necessary for the animator's job?" he asked.

We told **him**[5] that we already knew of artists who practically lived with deer to learn **their**[6] movements.

"The animators draw the extreme movements," **he**[7] continued, "but the inbetweeners make all the intermediate drawings. Finally, **it**[8] is the cleanup artist **who**[9] draws the most carefully of all. **Those**[10] who redraw, must add the final touches. For example," he said, as he pointed at a pig's suspenders, "these two buttons must be added at cleanup. It is the cleanup artist **whose**[11] work will be seen by **you**[12], the audience."

1. We – Pronoun: A personal pronoun replaces one or more nouns. OR "We" is a subjective pronoun; "our" is a possessive pronoun.
2. our – Pronoun: "Our" is a possessive pronoun; "us" is a subjective pronoun.
3. all – Pronoun: An indefinite pronoun does not refer to a specific person or thing. Indefinite pronouns are often used to make general statements or to indicate quantity.
4. you – Pronoun: Use a subjective personal pronoun.
5. him – Pronoun: "Him" is an objective pronoun; "he" is a subjective pronoun.
6. their – Pronoun: "Their" is a possessive pronoun; "them" is an objective pronoun.
7. he – Pronoun: "He" is a subjective pronoun; "his" is a possessive pronoun.
8. it – Pronoun: "It" is a subjective pronoun; "our" is a possessive pronoun.
9. who – Pronoun: "Who" is a subjective pronoun; "whom" is an objective pronoun.
10. those – Pronoun: "These" is nearby; "those" is farther away.
11. whose – Pronoun: Use a possessive pronoun to show ownership.
12. you – Pronoun: A subjective personal pronoun replaces one or more nouns (audience).

**38. Footnotes in Anatomy** (p. 69)

"Next, we're going to discuss the human foot, which has 26 bones in **all**[1]," said Mrs. Langdon. **"They**[2] can be divided into three different kinds." As she pointed at the ankle, Mrs. Langdon asked, "Can **anyone**[3] give the name for the ankle bones?" Becky answered that they were the tarsals. "That's right," Mrs. Langdon said. "The foot has seven tarsal bones. What about the instep bones?" Miguel correctly identified **them**[4] as the metatarsals. **"That's**[5] right again," Mrs. Langdon said. "The foot has five metatarsal bones. **Who**[6] knows what we call the bones in **our**[7] toes?" **Nobody**[8] knew, except Mrs. Langdon **herself**[9], so she continued. "The toe bones are called phalanges. The foot has fourteen phalanges. Two are in the big toe, and three are in **each**[10] of the other four toes. Can **anybody**[11] guess why the big toe has one fewer bone than the rest of the toes? Oh, there's the bell. We'll have to take up that subject on Monday. Have a great weekend!"

1. all – Pronoun: Use an indefinite to indicate quantity.
2. They – Pronoun: "They" is a subjective pronoun; "them" is an objective pronoun.
3. anyone – Pronoun: Use an indefinite pronoun to make general statements.
4. them – Pronoun: "Them" is an objective

pronoun; "they" is a subjective pronoun.

5. That's – Pronoun: When used alone (not modifying an noun), *this*, *that*, *these*, and *those* function as nouns and are considered demonstrative pronouns.
6. Who – Pronoun: "Who" is a subjective pronoun; "whom" is an objective pronoun.
7. our – Pronoun: Possessive pronouns show ownership and never need apostrophes.
8. Nobody – Pronoun: An indefinite pronoun does not refer to a specific person or thing. Indefinite pronouns are often used to make general statements or to indicate quantity.
9. herself – Pronoun: A pronoun antecedent must match the thing it replaces (Mrs. Langdon).
10. each – Pronoun: Use an indefinite pronoun to indicate quantity.
11. anybody – Pronoun: Use an indefinite pronoun to make general statements.

**39. Predators Beware** (p. 78)

The llama is a relative of the camel. Although the llama **has**[1] many similarities to the camel, the most noticeable difference between the two **is**[2] that the llama doesn't have a hump on its back. In South American countries, llamas are often **used**[3] as pack animals. In the U.S., people are **finding**[4] other uses for llamas. Some sheep ranchers **use**[5] llamas to guard their flocks. Llamas **graze**[6] in the fields with the sheep and **think**[7] of them as their herd. If the sheep are **attacked**[8], a llama **will rush**[9] at the attacker and strike with its large feet. It will also spit saliva into the attacker's face.

"Llamas are effective as the sheep's protectors," says rancher Giselle Robinson, "because they **reduce**[10] the number of sheep lost to predators. Overall, I'd say that we get along with llamas extremely well."

1. has – Verb: The action is happening now, so use the simple present tense of the verb.
2. is – Verb: The action is happening now, so use the simple present tense of the verb.
3. used – Verb: Add **-d** to the regular verb "use" to form the past tense.
4. finding – Verb: The action is continuing, so use the present progressive tense of the verb.
5. will use – Verb: The action is happening now, so use the simple present tense.
6. graze – Verb: Use the base infinitive of the verb in the active voice of the present tense.
7. think – Verb: The action is happening now, so use the simple present tense.
8. attacked – Verb: Use the past participle of the verb in the passive voice of the present tense.
9. will rush – Verbs: Use the active voice of the future tense.
10. reduce – Verbs: Use the active voice of the present tense.

**40. Camera Shy** (p. 79)

A hammerhead shark objected to having its photograph **taken**[1] and sent two scuba divers **swimming**[2] for cover. The divers, scientists with the National Oceanographic Society, **were taking**[3] pictures for an upcoming article featuring the hammerhead's uniquely shaped head. After slowly circling the divers, the shark suddenly tried **to butt**[4] them with its head. Bob Noble, the diver **armed**[5] with a shark dart, **made**[6] it into the diving cage first. Brian Black, the second diver, **dropped**[7] both his camera and his flipper as he **swam**[8] to safety. If the shark **swam**[9] faster than Noble and Black, they might not have been so lucky. Hammerhead sharks have **been**[10] known to attack people, and the scientists **were leaving**[11] nothing to chance. "Next time, **we will get**[12] his permission first," said the shaken Mr. Black.

1. taken – Verb: Use the past participle of the irregular verb.
2. swimming – Verb: Use the present participle.
3. were taking – Verb: Use the past tense of the verb "be" plus the present participle to form the past progressive.
4. to butt – Verb: Add "to" in front of the base form make it the infinitive.
5. armed – Verb: Use the past participle as an adjective.
6. made – Verb: Use the irregular verb in the simple past tense of the active voice.
7. dropped – Verb: Use the regular verb in the simple past tense of the active voice.
8. swam – Verb: Use the irregular verb in the simple past tense of the active voice.
9. swam – Verb: Subjunctive mood suggests

something hypothetical.

10. have been known – Verb: Use the past participle with the helping verb and the past participle in the verb phrase in the present perfect tense in the passive voice.
11. were leaving – Verb: Use the past tense form of the infinitive "to be" to form the past progressive tense.
12. we will get – Verb: Use the helping verb "will" to form the simple future tense.

**41. The Giant of His Age** (p. 80)

Leonardo da Vinci was a painter, a sculptor, a mathematician, a scientist, an engineer, a philosopher, and many other things. He was **known**[1] in popular culture for his paintings, including many that are still widely **recognized**[2]. His most famous painting was the Mona Lisa. In his day, he **was**[3] known for providing early models of technological advances that **included**[4] the airplane, the automobile, and the parachute. He also **proposed**[5] using simple machines, such as pulleys and levers, to **do**[6] complex tasks. One of his ideas was the wheel-driven machine, which **used**[7] the turning of a wheel to produce energy. During the Industrial Revolution, factories **began**[8] using this wheel-driven technology to produce hydroelectric power. In addition, da Vinci was famous for his enormous number of drawings of the human body, including illustrations of the functions of bones and organs. His drawings **were**[9] considered to be the first accurate portrayals of human anatomy. Because of the many contributions to our progress, da Vinci was a man to whom we **do owe**[10] many thanks.

1. was known – Verb: Use the past participle of the irregular verb to form the past tense of the passive voice.
2. are … recognized – Verb: Use the past participle of the word "recognize."
3. was – Verb: Use the correct form of the verb "be" in the past tense of the passive voice.
4. included – Verb: Add **-ed** to the regular verb "include" to form the past tense.
5. proposed – Verb: Add **-d** to the regular verb "propose" to form the past tense.
6. to do – Verb: Use the infinitive.
7. used – Verb: Add **-d** to the regular verb "use" to form the past tense.
8. began – Verb: Use the simple past tense of the irregular verb "begin."
9. were – Verb: Use the correct form of the helping verb "be" in this verb phrase in the past tense of the passive voice.
10. do owe – Verb: Use "do" in the present emphatic tense.

**42. The Gentle Sea Cow** (p. 81)

The manatee, or sea cow, **is**[1] the only herbivorous mammal that **lives**[2] entirely in the water. The manatee can grow to be 14 feet long and can weigh up to 1,500 pounds. Manatees **graze**[3] on underwater plants and can stay underwater for up to 30 minutes. The upper lip of the manatee **is divided**[4] into two parts. It **uses**[5] these two halves as pinchers to grab water plants. It can **eat**[6] more than 100 pounds of plants per day! The manatee likes warm coastal waters and, in the U.S., **inhabits**[7] the bays and rivers of Florida. In some parts of Florida and South America, manatees **are used**[8] to keep waterways free of weeds. The gentle manatee **is**[9] an endangered species. The encyclopedia article "Sea Cows," in fact, reports that one manatee, the Stellar's sea cow, was **hunted**[10] to extinction twenty-seven years after it was discovered!

1. is – Verb: Use the correct form of the linking verb "be" in the present tense.
2. ~~will~~ lives – Verb: Do not use a helping verb in the present tense of the active voice
3. ~~do~~ graze – Verb: Do not use "do" in present tense.
4. is divided – Verb: Use the helping verb "is" with the past participle in the present tense of the passive voice.
5. uses – Verb: Use the present tense of the active voice.
6. can eat – Verb: Use the helping verb "can" with the irregular verb to form a verb phrase.
7. inhabits – Verb: Use the regular verb in the present tense of the active voice.
8. are used – Verb: To form past tense, add **-d** to the regular verb "use" with a helping verb to form the verb phrase.
9. is – Verb: Use the correct form of the linking verb "be" in the present tense.
10. was hunted – Verb: Use the past participle

 

in the past tense of the passive voice.

**43. Night Fright** (p. 85)

**Deep in the night,**[1] she heard the sound of water roaring through the hallway. Saraya peeked out her door. The hallway was as dry now as it had been when she arrived earlier that day. It was even deeper in the night when she heard the horrible scream. She called **out,**[2] and her voice echoed in the silence. It was almost **dawn,**[3] for the sun was trying to **rise,**[4] when she felt her bed shake. She **jumped up;**[5] she threw open the door and ran into the hall. **Trying to ignore the intensifying screech behind her,**[6] she zoomed down the long stairway and into the courtyard. She considered climbing over **the ashlar wall that surrounded the castle,**[7] but decided against it. Frantic, she ran along the wall until she stumbled and fell. She heard the noise right **behind her,**[8] and then she turned around to face her fate. There stood her **brother,**[9] who had a big grin on his **face,**[10] holding a cell phone that was playing "Sounds in the Night."

"That's not fair, Mohammed!" Saraya cried. Mohammed just laughed. "We'll leave tomorrow. You'll see," Saraya said, planning to ask Mom and Dad to cut the visit short.

1. Deep in the night, – Phrase: When a phrase begins a sentence, it is followed by a comma.
2. out, – Clause: Put a comma after the first clause when two independent clauses are joined by a coordinating conjunction.
3. dawn, – Clause: Put a comma before the nonessential clause: for the sun was trying to rise.
4. rise, – Clause: Put a comma after the nonessential clause: for the sun was trying to rise.
5. jumped up; – Clause: Put a semicolon after the first clause because the clauses are not joined by a coordinating conjunction.
6. Trying to . . . behind her, – Phrase: When a phrase begins a sentence, it is usually followed by a comma.
7. ... the ashlar wall that surrounded the castle, – Misplaced Modifier: Now it is clear the wall was made of ashlar and that it surrounded the castle.
8. behind her, – Clause: Put a comma after the first clause because the two independent clauses are joined by a coordinating conjunction.
9. brother, – Clause: Put a comma before the nonessential clause: who had a big grin on his face.
10. face, – Clause: Put a comma after the nonessential clause: who had a big grin on his face.

**44. The Monarch** (p. 86)

**In the spring,**[1] butterflies seem to be **everywhere,**[2] but where do they live during the winter? In autumn, flocks of North American monarch butterflies migrate **south to**[3] milder climates. One of their destinations is Pacific Grove, **California,**[4] where they will remain until spring. They hibernate in trees in the parks and surrounding areas. **In some areas,**[5] special butterfly habitats have been set aside to protect these yearly visitors. When you **visit these habitats, you see what look like large clusters of dried leaves hanging from the trees.**[6] **In fact,**[7] these clusters are hundreds of butterflies with their wings closed. The dull under part of the monarch's wing resembles a dead **leaf;**[8] it provides the butterfly with protective camouflage when it is resting. The butterflies hang down in overlapping **layers from**[9] the tree branches. They will hibernate this way until spring arrives. When the butterflies' wings are warmed by the **sun,**[10] they will begin to fly again.

1. In the spring, – Phrase: When a phrase begins a sentence, it is usually followed by a comma.
2. everywhere, – Clause: Put a comma after the first clause when two independent clauses are joined by a coordinating conjunction.
3. south to – Phrase: A phrase must always be part of a sentence.
4. California, – Clause: Put a comma in front of the essential clause: where they ... spring.
5. In some areas, – Phrase: When a phrase begins a sentence, it is usually followed by a comma.
6. ... visit these habitats, you see what .... – Misplaced Modifier: Now this is clear the

habitats are not hanging from the trees.

7. In fact, – Phrase: When a phrase begins a sentence, it is usually followed by a comma.
8. leaf; – Clause: Put a semicolon after the first clause when two clauses are not joined by a coordinating conjunction.
9. layers from – Phrase: A phrase must always be part of a sentence.
10. sun, – Clause: When a dependent clause is followed by an independent clause, use a comma after the dependent clause.

**45. A Sucker for Squid** (p. 87)

A hidden video camera finally **captured the**[1] thief who'd been stealing the octopus food. **Over the last few days,**[2] a lab assistant had noticed something strange. Each morning, pieces of squid were **missing from**[3] the jar of food kept near the octopus tank. One night, he set up a **hidden video camera in a light fixture to monitor**[4] the lab. **The next day,**[5] the mystery was solved. The octopus had found a small opening in the cover of its tank. **During the night,**[6] it would squeeze through the opening. **Like all octopuses,**[7] it was able to compress all of its body except the mouth. **Fortunately for the octopus, the opening was large enough for its mouth to fit through.**[8] It slid its tentacles **through first,**[9] and then it pulled the rest of its body through the opening. Using the suckers on its arms, the octopus had then grasped the lid of the jar, pulled it off, removed a piece of squid, and proceeded to snack. When it was done **eating,**[10] the octopus climbed **back inside**[11] the tank.

1. captured the – Clause: A dependent clause has to be combined with an independent clause to form a sentence.
2. Over the last few days, – Phrase: When a phrase begins a sentence, it is usually followed by a comma.
3. 3 missing from – Clause: A dependent clause has to be combined with an independent clause to form a sentence.
4. … hidden video camera in a light fixture to monitor … . – Misplaced Modifier: Now this is clear the camera was in the light fixture.
5. The next day, – Phrase: When a phrase begins a sentence, it is usually followed by a comma.
6. During the night, – Phrase: When a phrase begins a sentence, it is usually followed by a comma.
7. Like all octopuses, – Phrase: When a phrase begins a sentence, it is usually followed by a comma.
8. Fortunately for the octopus, – Phrase: When a phrase begins a sentence, it is usually followed by a comma.
9. through first, – Clause: Put a comma after the first clause when two independent clauses are joined by a coordinating conjunction.
10. eating, – Clause: Use a comma when a dependent clause is followed by an independent clause.
11. back inside – Phrase: A phrase must always be part of a sentence.

**46. Heart-Racing Journey** (p. 88)

With the goal of studying a microscopic **society,**[1] I prepare for transport. I am successfully **shrunk,**[2] but something has gone wrong with the coordinates! I **materialize in**[3] the right atrium of a chambered muscular organ. What could have happened? Suddenly, **all is still,**[4] and I brace for a contraction. The jolt hurls the blood cells and me past the tricuspid valve into the right ventricle. Hey, I have somehow survived! The ventricle squeezes the blood and me toward the **lungs**[5] where I can be saved. Our engineer will surely locate and beam me **out once I'm there.**[6] I am propelled with a rush but slow down just at the pulmonary valve. **While I am struggling**[7] to escape, the three cusps trap me like doors! I am not to be defeated, though. **With a mighty effort,**[8] I pull my hips through and then my legs, too. I am free of the heart! I glide to the **lungs;**[9] I am sure that I will soon be saved.

1. society – Phrase: When a phrase begins a sentence, it is usually followed by a comma.
2. shrunk – Clause: Put a comma after the first clause when two independent clauses are joined by a coordinating conjunction.
3. materialize in – Phrase: A phrase must always be part of a sentence.

4. all is still, – Clause: Put a comma after the first clause when two independent clauses are joined by a coordinating conjunction.
5. lungs where – Clause: A dependent clause has to be combined with an independent clause to form a sentence.
6. out once I'm there – Clause: A dependent clause has to be combined with an independent clause to form a sentence.
7. While I am struggling – Dangling modifer: Now this is clear that "I" is struggling.
8. With a mighty effort, – Phrase: When a phrase begins a sentence, it is usually followed by a comma.
9. lungs; – Clause: Use a semicolon after the independent clause when a dependant clause follows.

**47. The Eagle Nebula** (p. 89)

As **I**[1] clicked through the television channels, **my**[2] favorite science show **appeared**[3]. "The **Hubble Space Telescope**[4], launched **in** 1990, has recorded many astounding images for **everyone**[5] on Earth," the announcer was saying. "One such image **is**[6] this picture of the Eagle Nebula, inside the Milky Way **galaxy."**[7] A brilliant vision of the nebula **filled**[8] my screen as he continued. "Radiation from nearby stars causes these enormous **towers of**[9] gas and dust to glow. **Notice**[10] the globules of gas at the top of the leftmost tower. **Each glob**[11], which is about the size of our solar system, may contain newly forming stars!" Wow! Where else could I learn as much as I **do from**[12] "Outer Visions"?

1. I – Pronoun: "I" is a subjective pronoun; "me" is an objective pronoun.
2. my – Pronoun: "My" is a possessive pronoun; "I" is a subjective pronoun.
3. appeared – Verb: Add **-ed** to the regular verb "appear" to form the past tense.
4. The Hubble Space Telescope… was saying. – Misplaced modifier: Now this is clear the Hubble Space Telescope was launched (not that the announcer was launched).
5. everyone – Pronoun: Use an indefinite pronoun to make general statements.
6. is – Verb: Use the correct form of the linking verb "be" in the present tense.
7. One such… galaxy – Misplaced modifier: Now this is clear the Eagle Nebula is inside the Milky Way (not that the image is inside the Milky Way).
8. filled – Verb: Add **-ed** to the regular verb "fill" to form the past tense.
9. towers of – Phrase: A phrase must always be part of a sentence
10. Notice – Verb: The action is happening now, so use the simple present tense of the verb.
11. Each glob… stars! – Misplaced modifier: Now this is clear that each glob is about the size of our solar system (not the stars are about the size of our solar system).
12. do from – Phrase: A phrase must always be part of a sentence.

**48. America's First Colony** (p. 90)

Jamestown, **founded in 1607,**[1] was the first permanent English colony in America. A group of English investors formed the London Company to seek profit in the new land. **They**[2] sent Capt. John Smith and a group of settlers to establish a colony in what is now Virginia. The new settlers **struggled**[3] with hunger, disease, and **attacks by**[4] the natives. The greatest of these threats to the little settlement's survival was disease. **Even with**[5] the arrival of two additional groups of **settlers,**[5] the population declined. The settlers **were**[6] determined, however, to survive. Many were indentured servants for **whom**[7] there was no going back. They had sold **their**[8] **labor in exchange for free passage to the new land.**[9] Four years after the founding, the London Company gave each colonist a parcel of land. **Many**[10] of the colonists started raising tobacco. This **proved**[11] to be a very profitable crop, and the colony finally **began**[12] to thrive.

1. founded in 1607, – Clause: Put a comma after the nonessential clause.
2. They – Pronoun: "They" is a subjective prounoun; "them" is an objective pronoun.
3. struggled – Verb: Add **-d** to the regular verb "struggle" to form the past tense.
4. attacks by - Phrase: A phrase must always be part of a sentence.
5. Even with…. settlers, – Clause: dependent clause + independent – Use a comma after

the dependent clause.

6. were – Verb: Use the irregular verb in the past tense of the passive voice.
7. whom – Pronoun: "Whom" is an objective pronoun; "who" is a subjective pronoun.
8. Their – Pronoun: "Their" is a possessive pronoun; "them" is an objective pronoun.
9. labor ... new land – Misplaced modifier: Now it is clear that their labor was sold in exchange for free passage (not sold to the land).
10. Many – Pronoun: An indefinite pronoun is often used to make general statements or to indicate quantity.
11. proved – Verb: Add **-d** to the regular verb "prove" to form past tense.
12. began – Verb: Use the irregular verb in the past tense of the active voice.

**49. Let the Chips Fall** (p. 94)

Harold is getting ready to bake a batch of cookies for Lisa to take to the carnival. He finds a recipe for chocolate chip cookies and **reads**[1] it thoughtfully. Harold **decides**[2] to add more chocolate chips and less flour so that the cookies will taste even better. He **doubles**[3] the amount of chips and halves the flour. He puts one cup of flour into the bowl and adds the other dry ingredients. He carefully breaks and adds the two eggs and mixes in the remaining ingredients. He spoons the batter onto a greased cookie sheet and **lays**[4] the sheet in the oven to bake for the required ten minutes. He takes the cookies out of the oven when the timer goes off. The cookies **are**[5] melted chocolate blobs. "Well, I can't **send**[6] **these**[7] cookies to the carnival. Surely, nobody **wants**[8] these," says Harold, "but **they**[9] won't go to waste." Harold knows to whom **he**[10] will give the chocolate mass. "By tonight, Lisa will have tasted my new recipe for chocolate candy!"

1. reads – Agreement: The number of the subject is not affected by any phrases that fall between the subject and the verb. (He ... reads)
2. decides – Agreement: Use a singular verb with a singular subject.
3. doubles – Agreement: Use a singular verb with a singular subject.
4. lays – Agreement: The number of the subject is not affected by any phrases that fall between the subject and the verb. (He ... lays)
5. are – Agreement: Use a plural verb with a plural subject.
6. send – Agreement: Verbs used with "I" do not end in s.
7. these cookies – Agreement: When *this*, *that*, *these*, or *those* are used as adjectives, they must agree in number with the noun they are modifying.
8. nobody wants – Agreement: Singular indefinite pronouns use a singular verb.
9. they – Agreement: A pronoun must agree with its antecedent (cookies) in number.
10. he – Agreement: A pronoun must agree with its antecedent (Harold) in person.

**50. The Treasure Hunters** (p. 95)

Carmen and Yoko had just read the story "The Treasure Hunters" in the best-selling book *Secrets of Lost Treasures*. **This morning**[1], **they**[2] wanted to play the board game with Anna and me. "We'll play," I said. "if **you give**[3] us a head start of five squares."

"Well, okay," Carmen conceded. "Who's ready to start?" Even though we had a 5-square head start, by 9:00 a.m. Carmen and Yoko had gotten **their**[4] scuba gear, passed the danger zones, and landed two moves from the treasure chest entrance. Things **weren't**[5] looking too good for us. It would have taken more than luck for us to get out of Big Brig and swipe the goods. Anna and I lost the game just as we expected. **Some of the games we play are**[6] just easier to win than others. **This game**[7] was clearly **our**[8] worst game ever. Oh well, I guess **you win**[9] some and you lose some!

1. This morning – Agreement: When *this*, *that*, *these*, or *those* are used as adjectives, they must agree in number with the noun (morning) they are modifying.
2. they – Agreement: A pronoun must agree with its antecedent (Carmen and Yoko) in number, gender, and person.
3. you give – Agreement: Use a plural verb

with "you."

4. their – Agreement: A possessive pronoun must agree with its antecedent (Carmen and Yoko).
5. weren't – Agreement: Use a plural verb with a plural subject.
6. Some ... are – Agreement: Depending on the subject, these words may be singular or plural: some, any, none, all, and most. "Games" is a plural subject and uses a plural verb.
7. This game – Agreement: When *this*, *that*, *these*, or *those* are used as adjectives, they must agree in number with the noun (game) they are modifying.
8. our – Agreement: A pronoun must agree with its antecedent (Anna and I) in number, gender, and person.
9. you win – Agreement: Verbs used with "you" do not end in s.

**51. Armchair Adventure** (p. 96)

"Did **you know**[1] that a geyser is like a pot bubbling over on the stove?" Brandon asked **his**[2] sister. "Boiling water expands into steam, and the water and steam **explode**[3] out of the geyser's mouth. It says here that minerals in the water **form**[4] cones or even towers around the mouth of a geyser."

"I already know all that," said Becky, "because **our**[5] aunt has been to Yellowstone National Park, Wyoming, with **her**[6] husband."

"She went with whom?" interrupted Brandon.

"She went with Uncle Earl," Becky answered impatiently, "and they also went to New Zealand and saw geysers right from their hotel room ."

"Wow!" said Brandon. "Maybe they'll take you and me next time."

Brandon hoped to see the sights shown in the magazine he **was**[7] reading. How about you? Would **you like**[8] to see the places in "Hot Spots: Great Geysers of the World?"

1. you know – Agreement: Verbs used with "you" do not end in s.
2. his – Agreement: A pronoun must agree with its antecedent (Brandon) in number, gender, and person.
3. explode – Agreement: Subjects joined with "and" take a plural verb.
4. form – Agreement: The number of the subject is not affected by any phrases that fall between the subject and the verb. (minerals... form)
5. our – Agreement: A possessive pronoun must agree with its antecedent (Brandon and Becky).
6. her – Agreement: A pronoun must agree with its antecedent (aunt) in number, gender, and person.
7. he was – Agreement: Use a singular verb with a singular subject.
8. you like – Agreement: Verbs used with "you" do not end in s.

**52. On the Loose** (p. 97)

Emmet Levison, zookeeper, **recalls**[1] the days of transporting animals by train. **He**[2] reminisces about one day in particular that turned out to be a very exciting one. "Once, a train carrying a shipment of ours derailed and let thirty animals go free. Most of the beasts **were**[3] rounded up, but an elusive tiger had fled to a nearby backyard. After he **was**[4] tranquilized, the big cat slumped into a patch of berries and could not even rise onto his feet." Emmet added that none of those animals **were**[5] injured or lost, but that the zoo administrator and **he**[6] **were**[7] worried. Emmet **remembers**[8] saying, "Now that these animals **have**[9] tasted freedom, we can't be sure **we**[10] could recapture them if this should ever happen again."

1. recalls – Agreement: Use a singular verb with a singular subject.
2. He – Agreement: A pronoun must agree with its antecedent (Emmett Levison) in number, gender, and person.
3. were – Agreement: Depending on the subject, these words may be singular or plural: some, any, none, all, and most. "Beasts" is a plural subject and uses a plural verb.
4. he was – Agreement: Use a singular verb with a singular subject.
5. were – Agreement: Depending on the subject, these words may be singular or plural: some, any, none, all, and most.

"Animals" is a plural subject.

6. he – Agreement: A pronoun must agree with its antecedent (Emmett Levison) in number, gender, and person.
7. were – Agreement: Depending on the subject, these words may be singular or plural: some, any, none, all, and most. "Animals" is a plural subject and uses a plural verb.
8. remembers – Agreement: Use a singular verb with a singular subject.
9. animals have – Agreement: Use a plural verb with a plural subject.
10. We – Agreement: A pronoun must agree with its antecedent (zoo staff) in number, gender, and person.

**53. Bales of Fun** (p. 100)

Rural Route 1
Canton, NY 13617
June 11, 2010

Dear Pham,

I'll bet your city is very exciting, but believe me, living in rural St. Lawrence County **can**[1] be great. We are located northwest of Lake Ontario between the Adirondack Mountains and Canada. My sister and I work here on a dairy farm and **learn**[2] something every day from our chores. At milking time, I spread the straw while Cindy **brings**[3] pails of milk to me in the barn. When we do the haying, Cindy picks up bales weighing a hundred pounds each and will **lay**[4] them onto the wagon. She just doesn't **quit**[5]! While drinking iced tea, I drive the tractor pulling the wagon. **Then**[6] at the barn, I watch the bales **rise**[7] to the loft on the hay elevator. I **let**[8] Cindy have the honor of catching and neatly stacking the bales in the 100° heat of the barn. The **effect**[9] is it's a great life for her and me! I don't understand why Cindy **can't**[10] wait to go to college in the city.

Sincerely,
Manuel

1. can – Confused words: Can is a verb that means to be able to. May is a verb that means to be permitted.
2. learn – Confused words: Learn is a verb that means to gain knowledge or understanding. Teach is a verb that means to instruct.
3. brings – Confused words: Bring is a verb that means to carry something with oneself to a place. Take is a verb that means to carry to another place.
4. lay – Confused words: Lay is a verb that means to put or place something. Lie is a verb that means to rest or recline.
5. quit – Confused words: Quit is a verb that means to stop. Quiet is an adjective that means silence.
6. Then – Confused words: Then is an adverb that refers to at that time. Than is a conjunction used only to compare.
7. rise – Confused words: Rise is a verb that means to move from lower to higher. Raise is a verb that means to move something to a higher position, to elevate.
8. let – Confused words: Let is a verb that means to allow. Leave is a verb that means to go away.
9. effect – Confused words: Effect is a noun that means a result. Affect is a verb that means to influence.
10. can't ~~not~~ – Negative words: Use only one negative word to state a negative idea.

**54. How to Catch a Wave** (p. 101)

The first steps in **learning**[1] how to surf are balancing on the surfboard and paddling. To begin, **lie**[2] horizontally along the center of the board. To balance, place your feet close together on the board. Paddling is done with alternating left and right strokes. After you have paddled out, you should **then**[3] face the ocean and start looking for a wave that is **farther**[4] out. When you see a good wave, turn yourself and your board toward the beach and begin paddling as strong and fast as you **can**[5]. Arch your back to keep the nose of your board from going underwater, and the wave will give you a nice push. When you can **accept**[6] the force of the wave, you should **raise**[7] yourself up and place your feet sideways on the board. Keep your board **quite**[8] steady and just ahead of the breaking wave. Your knees should be bent, and your torso should be slightly forward. Now hang

**loose**[9], and **don't**[10] wipe out!

1. learning – Confused words: Learn is a verb that means to gain knowledge or understanding. Teach is a verb that means to instruct.
2. lie – Confused words: Lie is a verb that means to rest or recline. Lay is a verb that means to put or place something.
3. then – Confused words: Then is an adverb that refers to time. Than is a conjunction used only to compare.
4. farther – Confused words: Farther is an adverb that refers to length or distance. Further is an adverb that refers to time, degree, or quantity.
5. can – Confused words: Can is a verb that means to be able to. May is a verb that means to be permitted.
6. accept – Confused words: Accept is a verb that means to receive. Except is a preposition/conjunction that means to leave out.
7. raise – Confused words: Raise is a verb that means to move something to a higher position, to elevate. Rise is a verb that means to move from lower to higher.
8. quite – Confused words: Quite is an adverb that means truly or considerably. Quiet is an adjective that mean silence.
9. loose – Confused words: Loose is an adjective that means not tight. Lose is a verb that means to not win.
10. don't ~~not~~ – Negative words: Use only one negative word to state a negative idea.

**55. Schedule It!** (p. 102)

Did she like being disorganized? Did she enjoy doing homework when her friends asked, "**Can**[1] you go dancing?" No, she **didn't**[2]. On the other hand, she felt **quite**[3] overwhelmed with things to do. I have **hardly**[4] any time!

Her father, who was a good advisor, came to the rescue with an article called "Doing It All." He said, "Prioritize your activities, and then **let**[5] go of the things that matter the least. Schedule important things first, and fit the other stuff around them. **Accept**[6] it and you'll get **farther**[7]."

**Then,**[8] Juanita began penciling activities on her schedule. She managed to include at least one fun thing each day. On Thursdays, she would surf at 3:30 and **proceed**[9] to watch her favorite television show at 9:30. Instead of playing with her brother after doing dishes, she **can**[10] practice her music for 45 minutes. She was pleased as she closed her eyes that night. "Tomorrow," Juanita said, "things will be different!"

1. Can – Confused words: Can is a verb that means to be able to. May is a verb that means to be permitted.
2. didn't ~~hardly~~ – Negative words: Use only one negative word to state a negative idea.
3. quite – Confused words: Quite is an adverb that means truly or considerably. Quit is a verb that means to stop.
4. hardly ~~not~~ – Negative words: Use only one negative word to state a negative idea. Take out either hardly or scarcely.
5. let – Confused words: Let is a verb that means to allow. Leave is a verb that means to go away.
6. Accept – Confused words: Accept is a verb that means to receive. Except is a preposition/conjunction that means to leave out.
7. farther – Confused words: Farther is an adverb that refers to length or distance. Further is an adverb that refers to time, degree, or quantity.
8. Then – Confused words: Then is an adverb that refers to time. Than is a conjunction used only to compare.
9. proceed – Confused words: Proceed is a verb that means to go forward. Precede is a verb that means to come before.
10. can – Confused words: Can is a verb that means to be able to. May is a verb that means to be permitted.

**56. Stained Glass** (p. 103)

As visitors to a prominent window maker, we are honored to be given a tour by the owner. "At Stained Panes, Inc.," President Cutler explains, "the art of constructing stained glass windows has been carefully preserved. The **effect**[1] of our final products is great because they are made with special glass imported from Europe. We **teach**[2] students to cut plain glass first. Would you like to watch one of our apprentices?" We look on as he says to the student, "For now, you **can**[3] make a straight cut. You must **lay**[4] the glass cutter down and apply pressure as you roll it along a straight guide to the end then **quit**[5]. **Proceed**[6] using the glass pliers to separate the two pieces of glass. Finally, **raise**[7] the piece to see how you've done." **Then**[8] Mr. Cutler says, "Next time, we'll try some curves. Stained glass **isn't,**[9] an easy craft to perfect, but you will know it is worthwhile when you see the sun **rise**[10] through a window of red and gold German glass."

1. effect – Confused words: Effect is a noun that means a result. Affect is a verb that means to influence.
2. teach – Confused words: Teach is a verb that means to instruct. Learn is a verb that means to gain knowledge or understanding.
3. can – Confused words: May is a verb that means to be permitted. Can is a verb that means to be able to.
4. lay – Confused words: Lie is a verb that means to rest or recline. Lay is a verb that means to put or place something.
5. quit – Confused words: Quiet is an adjective that mean silence. Quit is a verb that means to stop.
6. Proceed – Confused words: Proceed is a verb that means to go forward. Precede is a verb that means to come before.
7. raise – Confused words: Raise is a verb that means to move something to a higher position, to elevate. Rise is a verb that means to move from lower to higher.
8. Then – Confused words: Then is an adverb that refers to at that time. Than is a conjunction used only to compare.
9. isn't ~~hardly~~ – Negative words: Use only one negative word to state a negative idea.
10. rise – Confused words: Rise is a verb that means to move from lower to higher. Raise is a verb that means to move something to a higher position, to elevate.

**57. The Burning Phoenix** (p. 106)

The phoenix was a bird in Greek and Egyptian **mythology. It**[1] was as large or larger than an eagle and had brilliant scarlet and gold **plumage. It**[2] had a melodious cry. Only **one phoenix**[3] existed at any time, and it was always **male. The**[4] Greek and Egyptian writers said he lived to **be five**[5] hundred years old. When the life cycle of the **phoenix came**[6] to a close, he would gather wood and other burnable items and light himself on **fire. Out**[7] of the ashes, a new phoenix would arise. The new phoenix would then **carry the**[8] ashes of his father to the sun god, Re, in Heliopolis (City of the Sun). Because of the long life span of the phoenix and his rebirth from the ashes, he **symbolized immortality**[9] and **rebirth. He**[10] was also said to symbolize the rising and setting of the sun.

1. mythology. It – Run-On Sentence: Replace "and" with a period and capitalize the first word of the new sentence.
2. plumage. It – Run-On Sentence: Replace "and" with a period and capitalize the first word of the new sentence.
3. one phoenix – Sentence Fragment: Remove the period at the end of the first fragment. Change the capital letter to lowercase on the first word of the second fragment.
4. male. The – Run-On Sentence: Replace "and" with a period and capitalize the first word of the new sentence.
5. be five – Sentence Fragment: Remove the period at the end of the first fragment. Change the capital letter to lowercase on the first word of the second fragment.
6. phoenix came – Sentence Fragment: Remove the period at the end of the first fragment. Change the capital letter to lowercase on the first word of the second fragment.
7. fire. Out – Run-On Sentence: Put a period after the first complete sentence and

 

capitalize the first word of the new sentence.

8. carry the – Sentence Fragment: Remove the period at the end of the first fragment. Change the capital letter to lowercase on the first word of the second fragment.
9. symbolized immortality – Sentence Fragment: Remove the period at the end of the first fragment. Change the capital letter to lowercase on the first word of the second fragment.
10. rebirth. He – Run-On Sentence: Replace "and" with a period and capitalize the first word of the new sentence.

**58. Uses of Peanut Oil** (p. 107)

Watch out if you have just eaten a peanut butter **sandwich. That**[1] snack of yours might **be more**[2] powerful than you think. The oil of peanuts is used for making nitroglycerin, an explosive ingredient of **dynamite. Peanut**[3] oil is also commonly used in household items. It can be **used to**[4] make soap by the process of saponification. It is safe for use as a massage **oil. In**[5] fact, in 1933, noted peanut researcher George Washington Carver **developed a**[6] peanut massage oil to treat polio. At the 1900 Paris Exhibition, the Otto Company, at the request of the French government, demonstrated that peanut oil could be used as a source of fuel for the diesel **engine; this**[7] was one of the earliest demonstrations of bio-diesel technology. Grooming products and paint **sometimes contain**[8] peanut oil. It is used in salad dressing, **too. Compared**[9] to olive oil, peanut oil is considered by some people to be **tastier. Indeed,**[10] peanut oil has many uses.

1. sandwich. That – Run-On Sentence: Put a period after the first complete sentence and capitalize the first word of the new sentence.
2. be more – Sentence Fragment: Remove the period at the end of the first fragment. Change the capital letter to lowercase on the first word of the second fragment.
3. dynamite. Peanut – Run-On Sentence: Replace "and" with a period and capitalize the first word of the new sentence.
4. used to – Sentence Fragment: Remove the period at the end of the first fragment. Change the capital letter to lowercase on the first word of the second fragment.
5. oil. In – Run-On Sentence: Replace "and" with a period and capitalize the first word of the new sentence.
6. developed a – Sentence Fragment: Remove the period at the end of the first fragment. Change the capital letter to lowercase on the first word of the second fragment.
7. engine; this – Run-On Sentence: Replace "and" with a semicolon.
8. sometimes contain – Sentence Fragment: Remove the period at the end of the first fragment. Change the capital letter to lowercase on the first word of the second fragment.
9. too. Compared – Run-On Sentence: Replace "and" with a period and capitalize the first word of the new sentence.
10. tastier. Indeed – Run-On Sentence: Replace "and" with a period and capitalize the first word of the new sentence.

**59. Ride the Wild River** (p. 108)

Rafting is a sport that **appeals to**[1] the adventurous athlete. It's like a roller coaster ride without the seat **belts. The**[2] beginning of our journey downriver was calm and uneventful. We entered the rapids more **abruptly than**[3] I had expected. The raft was lifted by a wave and dropped into a pool of swirling **water. The**[4] raft spun around several times before the guide could point it back downriver. Our paddles **were useless**[5] in the rushing water. We spent the rest of our **time bailing**[6] out all 13 feet of our raft as wave after wave came pouring over **us. We**[7] were so wet and chilly that we were shaking as we **finally pulled**[8] into shore for the **night. What**[9] an exhilarating day we'd had! Would we do it again **if we**[10] had the chance? You bet we would!

1. appeals to – Sentence Fragment: Remove the period at the end of the first fragment. Change the capital letter to lowercase on the first word of the second fragment.
2. belts. The – Run-On Sentence: Replace "and" with a period and capitalize the first

word of the new sentence.

3. abruptly than – Sentence Fragment: Remove the period at the end of the first fragment. Change the capital letter to lowercase on the first word of the second fragment.
4. water. The – Run-On Sentence: Replace "and" with a period and capitalize the first word of the new sentence.
5. were useless – Sentence Fragment: Remove the period at the end of the first fragment. Change the capital letter to lowercase on the first word of the second fragment.
6. time bailing – Sentence Fragment: Remove the period at the end of the first fragment. Change the capital letter to lowercase on the first word of the second fragment.
7. us. We – Run-On Sentence: Replace "and" with a period and capitalize the first word of the new sentence.
8. finally pulled – Sentence Fragment: Remove the period at the end of the first fragment. Change the capital letter to lowercase on the first word of the second fragment.
9. night. What – Run-On Sentence: Replace "and" with a period and capitalize the first word of the new sentence.
10. if we – Sentence Fragment: Remove the period at the end of the first fragment. Change the capital letter to lowercase on the first word of the second fragment.

**60. Birth of a Volcano** (p. 109)

Imagine that you are walking through a **cornfield. The**[1] day is fine, but you are a bit nervous because there have been a lot of earthquakes **lately; suddenly**[2], a crack opens in the ground and comes **racing toward**[3] you. Steam and sulfur gas rise from the crack and **carry the**[4] smell of rotten eggs. You run **away! Half**[5] an hour later you hear an explosion and see a black cloud rising high into the **air. These**[6] events could have happened to you if you had **been walking**[7] in the corn field 180 miles west of Mexico City, Mexico, on February 20, 1943, when the volcano Paricutin was born. Three weeks before the eruption actually occurred, rumbling noises that resembled **thunder were**[8] heard by people near Paricutin **Village; these**[9] were actually deep earthquakes. Like most cinder cone volcanoes, Paricutin is believed to be a monogenetic volcano, which means that once it has finished erupting it well never erupt **again. In**[10] 1952, Paricutin finished erupting and has been quiet ever since.

1. cornfield. The – Run-On Sentence: Replace "and" with a period and capitalize the first word of the new sentence.
2. lately; suddenly, – Run-On Sentence: Replace "and" with a semicolon.
3. racing toward – Sentence Fragment: Remove the period at the end of the first fragment. Change the capital letter to lowercase on the first word of the second fragment.
4. carry the – Sentence Fragment: Remove the period at the end of the first fragment. Change the capital letter to lowercase on the first word of the second fragment.
5. away! Half – Run-On Sentence: Replace "and" with an exclamation mark and capitalize the first word of the new sentence.
6. air. These – Run-On Sentence: Replace "and" with a period and capitalize the first word of the new sentence.
7. been walking – Sentence Fragment: Remove the period at the end of the first fragment. Change the capital letter to lowercase on the first word of the second fragment.
8. thunder were – Sentence Fragment: Remove the period at the end of the first fragment. Change the capital letter to lowercase on the first word of the second fragment.
9. Village; these – Run-On Sentence: Replace "and" with a semicolon.
10. again. In – Run-On Sentence: Put a period after the first complete sentence and capitalize the first word of the new sentence.

**61. Print Patterns** (p. 110)

Have you ever heard that **no**[1] two fingerprints are alike? Everyone has different fingerprint patterns. **These**[2] fingerprints are made up of a pattern of ridges that **vary in**[3] number, size, and location. There are three basic patterns of fingerprints: loops, whorls, and arches. The most commonly occurring of the three patterns **is**[4] the **loop. A**[5] loop must have one ridge that enters from one side, curves around, and exits from the same side. Whorls involve **ridges that**[6] curve in a circular pattern. The arch, the least common pattern, is formed by ridges that enter from one side, **rise**[7] in the middle, and **then**[8] exit. A print from the foot **can**[9] also leave an impression with **ridges. Be**[10] careful what you touch or where you walk!

1. ~~hardly~~ no – Negative words: Use only one negative word to state a negative idea.
2. These – Agreement: When *this*, *that*, *these*, or *those* are used as adjectives, they must agree in number with the noun they are modifying.
3. vary in – Sentence Fragment: Remove the period at the end of the first fragment. Change the capital letter to lowercase on the first word of the second fragment.
4. is – Agreement: The number of the subject is not affected by any phrases that fall between the subject and the verb.
5. loop. A – Run-On Sentence: Add a period and capitalize the first word of the new sentence.
6. ridges that – Sentence Fragment: Remove the period at the end of the first fragment. Change the capital letter to lowercase on the first word of the second fragment.
7. Rise – Confused words: Rise is a verb that means to move from lower to higher. Raise is a verb that means to move something to a higher position, to elevate.
8. Then – Confused words: Then is an adverb that refers to at that time. Than is a conjunction used only to compare.
9. can – Confused words: Can is a verb that means to be able to. May is a verb that means to be permitted.
10. ridges. Be – Run-On Sentence: Put a period after the first complete sentence and capitalize the first word of the new sentence.

**62. The Monkey in the Jeep** (p. 111)

You never know what will happen in the savannahs of Eastern Africa. In the country of Tanzania, a caravan of tired travelers **came upon**[1] a place to rest and take a break. Everyone wanted to go see the herd of elephants **that**[2] were close by, **except**[3] two of the travelers who stayed behind. They began to watch a small monkey walking toward the jeep. In a split second, **that**[4] monkey **proceeded**[5] to take off running and jumped in **the jeep. He**[6] **then**[7] grabbed the closest drink box and scampered up the nearest tree. **Both**[8] travelers were so surprised, yet excited, because they had been taking pictures the entire time the **monkey was**[9] racing in and out of the jeep. Soon **all**[10] the travelers returned only to **learn**[11] that they had missed **out. This**[12] had been a once in a lifetime experience for the two travelers and the monkey in the jeep!

1. came upon – Sentence Fragment: Remove the period at the end of the first fragment. Change the capital letter to lowercase on the first word of the second fragment.
2. that – Agreement: A pronoun must agree with its antecedent (elephants) in number, gender, and person.
3. except – Confused words: Accept is a verb that means to receive. Except is a preposition/conjunction that means to leave out.
4. that – Agreement: When *this*, *that*, *these*, or *those* are used as adjectives, they must agree in number with the noun or pronoun they are modifying.
5. proceeded – Confused words: Precede is a verb that means to come before. Proceed is a verb that means to go forward.
6. the jeep. He – Run-On Sentence: Add a period and capitalize the first word of the new sentence.
7. then – Confused words: Then is an adverb that refers to time. Than is a conjunction used only to compare.
8. Both – Agreement: A pronoun must agree with its antecedent (two travelers) in number,

gender, and person.

9. monkey was – Sentence Fragment: Remove the period at the end of the first fragment. Change the capital letter to lowercase on the first word of the second fragment.
10. all – Agreement: A pronoun must agree with its antecedent (travelers) in number, gender, and person.
11. learn – Confused words: Teach is a verb that means to instruct. Learn is a verb that means to gain knowledge or understanding.
12. out. This – Run-On Sentence: Add a period and capitalize the first word of the new sentence.

**63. Mammal Discovery** (p. 112)

**In the early 1990s,**[1] scientists **discovered**[2] two new species of mammals. **Both were**[3] found in the isolated and mountainous Vu Quang Nature Reserve in Vietnam. The Vu Quang ox, also known as a saola or Asian unicorn, **is**[4] an ox that has long horns and a dark brown coat with a black stripe along **its**[5] back. It weighs about 220 pounds. It is a distant relative to sheep and **cattle. It**[6] was the first new large mammal found in more than 50 years. It is a forest-dwelling bovine and **one of**[7] the world's rarest mammals. The giant muntjac, a deer with huge canine teeth, was discovered soon after the Vu Quange ox. It **has**[8] a reddish brown coat and **weighs**[9] between 66 and 110 pounds. The first live specimen **caught was**[10] a Vu Quang ox calf. It was sent to a botanical garden in Hanoi for study. The **effect**[11] of hunting, combined with slash and burn agriculture, **has caused**[12] the giant muntjac to be considered an endangered species. It is also preyed upon by animals such as the tiger and the leopard.

1. In the early 1990s, – Phrase: When a phrase begins a sentence, it is usually followed by a comma.
2. discovered – Verbs: Add **-ed** to the regular verb "discover" to form the past tense.
3. Both were – Agreement: Plural indefinite pronouns use a plural verb.
4. is – Agreement: The number of the subject is not affected by any phrases that fall between the subject and the verb. (Vu Quang ox... is)
5. its – Pronouns: Possessive pronouns show ownership and never need apostrophes. Some possessive pronouns are: mine, yours, his, hers, its, ours, theirs.
6. cattle. It – Run-On Sentence: Replace "and" with a period and capitalize the first word of the new sentence.
7. one of – Sentence Fragment: Remove the period at the end of the first fragment. Change the capital letter to lowercase on the first word of the second fragment.
8. has – Agreement: Use a singular verb with a singular subject.
9. weighs – Agreement: The number of the subject is not affected by any phrases that fall between the subject and the verb. (It... weighs)
10. caught was – Pronoun: Use a noun or a pronoun, but not both together, as the subject of a sentence.
11. effect – Confused words: Effect is a noun that means a result. Affect is a verb that means to influence.
12. has caused – Verbs: Use "has" plus the past participle of the word "cause" to form the verb phrase in the present perfect tense.

**64. Victory on Wheels** (p. 113)

Amy was fast that day. In fact, she **had never**[1] ridden faster. "She rides like the wind," her husband said as she whizzed by. She **had been leading**[2] the pack by more than 30 seconds. She thrust her fists in the air and yelled excitedly as she came across the finish line twenty-two seconds before the next finisher. It was her second **victory in**[3] a bicycle race.

**On the way home,**[4] she and her husband tried to decide what contributed to her great finish. "Was it what I ate?" she **asked**[5].

"Maybe **it was**[6] because you were well rested," he guessed.

They decided **that her**[7] success was probably a combination of all the possibilities, and that made it difficult to **duplicate. Anyway**[8], victory was **hers**[9]. **Looking to the future**[10] Amy's mind was already racing to the women's triathlon that would take place in three weeks. **Can**[11] she make it **her**[12] next victory?

1. had ~~hardly~~ never – Negative words: Use only one negative word to state a negative

idea.

2. had been leading – Verb: In the past perfect progressive tense, use "had" plus the past participle of "be" and the present participle "leading."
3. victory in – Sentence Fragment: Remove the period at the end of the first fragment. Change the capital letter to lowercase on the first word of the second fragment.
4. On the way home, – Phrase: Use a comma when a phrase begins a sentence.
5. asked – Verb: Add **-ed** to the regular verb "ask" to form the past tense.
6. it was – Agreement: Use a singular verb with a singular subject.
7. that her – Sentence Fragment: Remove the period at the end of the first fragment. Change the capital letter to lowercase on the first word of the second fragment.
8. duplicate. Anyway, – Run-On Sentence: Replace "and" with a period and capitalize the first word of the new sentence.
9. hers – Pronoun: Possessive pronouns show ownership and never need apostrophes.
10. Looking to the future, – Phrase: Use a comma when a phrase begins a sentence.
11. Can – Confused Words: Can is a verb that means to be able to. May is a verb that means to be permitted.
12. her – Agreement: A pronoun must agree with its antecedent (Amy) in number, gender, and person.

**65. Count on Computers** (p. 114)

We humans like to make things easy for **ourselves**[1]. **Because we have eight fingers and two thumbs,**[2] we use the decimal number system. It is based on ten digits. Computers, however, are more suited to the binary, or base two, **system. Base**[3] two requires only two symbols. A one or a zero **can easily be expressed in the computer**[4] as either a flow of electricity or no flow of electricity. How do **we read**[5] a number in base two? On the farthest right is the ones place. The next place to the left **is**[6] the twos place. The third place shows how many fours, the fourth place shows how many eights, and so on. **Then**[7] we add all the values **that**[8] hold ones to get the equivalent decimal number. Therefore, the binary number in the illustration **represents**[9] our decimal number twenty-one. **Since only two states of electric flow need to be used,**[10] the binary number system lets computers process information more easily **than**[11] they could otherwise. Computers, in turn, **can make**[12] things easier **for us**[13]. Awesome!

1. ourselves – Pronoun: Reflexive pronouns reflect back on an antecedent (we) that is within the same sentence.
2. Because ... thumbs, – Clause: When a sentence consists of a dependent clause followed by an independent clause, the dependent clause should be followed by a comma.
3. system. Base – Run-On Sentence: Replace "and" with a period and capitalize the first word of the new sentence.
4. can easily be expressed in the computer – Phrase: (Misplaced Modifier) This makes it clear the one or zero is expressed in the computer.
5. we read – Sentence Fragment: Remove the period at the end of the first fragment. Change the capital letter to lowercase on the first word of the second fragment.
6. is – Agreement: Use a singular verb with a singular subject.
7. Then – Confused Words: Then is an adverb that refers to time. Than is a conjunction used only to compare.
8. that – Pronoun: That refers to people, things, qualities, and ideas. Who refers only to people.
9. represents – Agreement: The number of the subject is not affected by any phrases that fall between the subject and the verb (number… represents)
10. Since ... used, – Clause: When a sentence consists of a dependent clause followed by an independent clause, the dependent clause should be followed by a comma.
11. than – Confused Words: Than is a conjunction used only to compare. Then is an adverb that refers to time.

12. can make – Verb: Use the helping verb "can" with the base form "make" in the active voice of the future tense.
13. for us – Pronoun: Do not use a reflexive pronoun, but a pronoun as the object of the sentence.

**66. An Archaeological Find** (p. 115)

Today, our exacting field work in Australia was **rewarded**[1]. We **spent**[2] most of the day carefully uncovering what seemed to be an ancient knife. We had many **questions. When**[3] was it made? Was it used as a weapon? Was **it used**[4] for cooking? Once the knife **was uncovered**[5], we noticed another object just below it. **It**[6] was a small wood carving in the shape of a dingo, a dog brought to Australia by the Aborigines about 5,000 to 8,000 years ago. We theorized that the **knife was**[7] most likely used to carve the wooden dog. However, we had no indication of the carving's age. We will **have**[8] to use the tree ring dating method to find out how old the carving actually is. Every wooden object **has**[9] tree rings. Each ring represents one **year of**[10] growth. We will compare the rings of the carving to the rings of a nearby tree to see where they match. **We are**[11] **eager to find out how old these artifacts really are**[12]. What more will we **learn**[13]?

1. rewarded – Verb: Use the past participle as an adjective.
2. spent – Verb: Use the irregular verb in the past tense.
3. questions. When – Run-On Sentence: Replace "and" with a period and capitalize the first word of the new sentence.
4. it used – Sentence Fragment: Remove the period at the end of the first fragment. Change the capital letter to lowercase on the first word of the second fragment.
5. was uncovered – Verb: Use the linking verb "was" with the past tense of "uncover" to show the passive voice.
6. It – Agreement: A pronoun must agree with its antecedent (carving) in number, gender, and person.
7. knife was – Sentence Fragment: Remove the period at the end of the first fragment. Change the capital letter to lowercase on the first word of the second fragment.
8. have – Verb: This is a verb phrase in the future tense of the active voice.
9. has – Agreement: Use a singular verb with a singular subject.
10. year of – Phrase: A phrase must always be part of a sentence.
11. We are – Pronoun: When a pronoun is used as the subject in a sentence, the verb must agree with the pronoun in number.
12. to find out how old these artifacts really are – Phrase: (Misplaced Modifier) This clearly emphasizes the age of the artifacts.
13. learn – Confused Words: Learn is a verb that means to gain knowledge or understanding. Teach is a verb that means to instruct.

**67. Close Call** (p. 116)

The day got off to a great start! It was springtime and the weather was perfect. So, Dakota and his wife Catori, decided to **pack the family**[1] into their **convertible**[2] and go for a Saturday afternoon drive in the forest. They were enjoying the beautiful scenery along **Forest Drive**[3], while listening to the tune **"Wild Nature."**[4] **Suddenly**[5], two deer appeared out of nowhere. **In order to avoid hitting the deer,**[6] Dakota ran the car in a **pine tree**[7]. Fortunately, no **one**[8] was hurt! Dakota **exclaimed**[9], "Wow! I've **never**[10] **seen**[11] animals appear so suddenly." It was a little scary for everyone since it happened so **unexpectedly. The**[12] doe and the fawn were the **most beautiful**[13] **deer**[14] they'd ever seen. They'll most likely never encounter those two again, but they'll sure have a beauty of a dent to remind them of those deer.

1. pack the family – Preposition: Do not use a preposition where it is not necessary.
2. convertible – Spelling: The root word is vert (L) – turn.
3. Forest Drive – Content: See caption.
4. "Wild Nature" – Punctuation: Use quotation marks to identify the title of a song.
5. Suddenly – Adverb: Use an adverb to describe how something happens. Many adverbs are formed by adding -ly to adjectives.
6. In... deer, – Clause: When a sentence consists of a dependent clause followed

by an independent clause, the dependent clause should be followed by a comma.

7. pine tree – Content: See picture and caption.
8. one – Spelling: (homophone) one is a single thing; won means finished first
9. exclaimed – Verb: Add **-ed** to the regular verb "exclaim" to form the past tense.
10. never – Negative Words: Use only one negative word to state a negative idea.
11. seen – Verb: Use the past participle of the irregular verb "see" in the present perfect tense.
12. unexpectedly. The – Run-On Sentence: Replace "and" with a period and capitalize the first word of the new sentence.
13. most beautiful – Adjectives: Add "most" before a superlative adjective with three syllables to compare three or more people or things.
14. deer – Spelling: Some words don't change form at all for the singular and plural.

**68. An Educational Trip** (p. 117)

529 Evergreen Court
Boise, ID 83704
July 8, 2007

Dear **Hiroshi,**[1]

My parents took my brother and **me**[2] to the seashore. **Neither my brother nor**[3] I had ever seen the ocean before. **Wow!**[4] It was really great. **There were seagulls**[5] all around the shore. We saw **a lot**[6] of plants and animals in the water, too. Did **you know**[7] that there are many kinds of seaweeds? Seaweeds can be brown, red, or green, They are all algae, and they attach **themselves**[8] to rocks. The part attached to the **rocks**[9] is called a **holdfast**[10], and small animals live in it. Animals live on the leaves, **too**[11]. One type of seaweed can grow a foot in a day, and some seaweeds grow to be very long. We saw a giant kelp that was **brown**[12] and almost 200 feet long! This trip sure did **teach**[13] us a lot!

**Sincerely,**[14]
Basha

1. Hiroshi, – Punctuation: Use a comma in a friendly letter after the greeting.
2. me – Pronouns: Use "me" when you are receiving the action.
3. Neither ... nor – Conjunction: Correlative conjunctions come in pairs and join similar concepts in a sentence together.
4. Wow! – Punctuation: Use an exclamation mark after a word or sentence that shows excitement, fear, joy, or other strong emotion.
5. There were seagulls – Agreement: Use a plural verb with a plural subject.
6. a lot – Spelling: "A lot" is always two words.
7. you know – Sentence Fragment: Remove the period at the end of the first fragment. Change the capital letter to lowercase on the first word of the second fragment.
8. themselves – Pronoun: A reflexive pronoun reflects back on an antecedent (they) that is within the same sentence.
9. rocks – Content: See caption.
10. holdfast – Content: See caption.
11. too – Spelling: (homophone) too means also; to means "in a direction toward"
12. brown – Content: See caption.
13. teach – Confused Words: Teach is a verb that means to instruct. Learn is a verb that means to gain knowledge or understanding.
14. Sincerely, – Capitalization: Capitalize the first word in the closing in a letter.

**69. Pangolins** (p. 118)

There are **a total**[1] of eight species of pangolin on our planet. Four of them live in Asia, and the other four live in Africa. Pangolins, also known as scaly anteaters, are unique creatures that are **covered**[2] in hard, overlapping **scales. They**[3] are **insectivorous**[4] **(feeding on insects)**[5] and are mainly nocturnal. Their name is derived from the **Malay**[6] word "pengguling," which loosely translates to "something that rolls up." They have large, **sharp**[7] claws that they use for excavating ant and termite nests, and also for pulling bark off trees and logs to locate their insect prey. Pangolins don't have teeth and are unable to chew. Instead, they have **long**[8], sticky tongues that they use to catch the insects they feed on. When a pangolin's tongue is fully **extended,**[9] **it**[10] can be up to 16 inches longer than its entire body length. It is **believed**[11] that a single **pangolin consumes**[12] more than 70 million insects per year. A **pangolin's**[13] diet consists mainly of ants and termites. **Pangolins**[14] have poor vision and hearing, but an excellent sense of smell.

1. a total – Article: Use **a** before a word that begins with a consonant sound.
2. covered – Verb: Use the past participle.
3. scales. They – Run-On Sentence: Replace "and" with a period and capitalize the first word of the new sentence.
4. insectivorous – Spelling: The root word is: vor (L) - eat
5. (feeding on insects) – Punctuation: Use parentheses to surround words or figures to make things clearer.
6. Malay – Capitalization: Capitalize a language.
7. sharp – Content: See caption.
8. long – Content: See caption.
9. extended, – Clause: When a sentence consists of a dependent clause followed by an independent clause, the dependent clause should be followed by a comma.
10. it – Agreement: A pronoun must agree with its antecedent (tongue) in number, gender, and person.
11. believed – Spelling: Drop the silent "e" from a word when adding a vowel suffix.
12. pangolin consumes – Sentence Fragment: Remove the period at the end of the first fragment. Change the capital letter to lowercase on the first word of the second fragment.
13. pangolin's – Punctuation: Use an apostrophe to form the possessive.
14. Pangolins – Spelling: Apostrophes are not necessary with the regular plurals of words.